MW01198860

Proven

Tips and Techniques Every Police Officer
Should Know

Jeremy Guida

First published by Dog Ear Publishing
4011 Vincennes Rd
Indianapolis, IN 46268
www.dogearpublishing.net

ISBN: 978-1-4575-5076-8

This book is printed on acid-free paper.

Printed in the United States of America

ACKNOWLEDGMENTS

A lot of thought and help has gone into writing this book. I want to thank my children first. While you may not remember all the hours Daddy spent typing away on the computer, it did come at a cost to you. Thank you for your understanding, and I will make up every minute I lost, I promise. I want to thank my wife, Jennifer. Even though the comments and jokes were a plenty, I know deep down inside you supported me, like you always do. I want to thank my brothers, Mackenze, Corey, and sister Taylor. Had it not been for the backyard wrestling matches and flying elbows off the roof, I might not have been tough enough to endure this job. I want to thank my grandparents, Jim and Donna. You took me in as your own son and imparted lessons on me that made me a better man. Without you, I wouldn't be the man I am today.

I want to thank some of the bravest most courageous men I know: My brother Justin, you have been with me from the womb until now, and there is nothing we have faced together that we have not overcome. To my friends Andrew, Bryan, and Mike Y., we have been through a lot together. We've learned together, we've had successes together, and we've had failures together. But what we've always done is come out on top with a lot of laughs in-between.

I want to thank all the new officers just starting out. Thank you for choosing this career. It's a fulfilling one, and you will have much success as we pass the torch to you.

Most of all, I want to thank all the men and women that put a badge on every day. Your dedication and sacrifice may go unnoticed to some, but it does not go unnoticed to all. May you stay safe in your careers and always serve with the utmost integrity that our badge deserves.

DISCLAIMER

Nothing in this book is intended to supersede any federal, state, city, or local law. Nor is it intended to supersede any departmental regulation, general order, SOP, or any provision. If you are unsure of the legality of any action you are about to take, don't take it. Consult with someone that has the pertinent information that you require and learn for the next time. Laws, procedures, etc., are always changing. Make sure you keep up with the updates in your jurisdictions. The information provided in this book is a guideline. You must never sacrifice the safety of your scene to deploy a tactic or technique that you are unsure of or are uncomfortable with.

CONTENTS

Part Three

INTRODUCTION

I can remember all the way back to middle school wanting to be a police officer. I don't know where the urge initially came from, but all I knew was that this is what I wanted to do. I wanted to serve the community and country that I loved so much. But most of all, I wanted to catch bad guys. As I moved through high school, I thought about how I would settle into law enforcement. I came up with the idea that I wanted to join the FBI and become a criminal profiler. I started to take criminal law classes, and I read every book I could get my hands on. The books that I was interested in were primarily focused on the behavioral analyses of serial killers. After I graduated high school, I got a scholarship to Canisius College in Buffalo, NY. I immediately knew that I wanted a dual major in criminal justice and psychology. I had always wanted to be a police officer, and I was fascinated with the internal workings of the human mind. I thought for the career that I was headed to that perspective would be invaluable. The summer before college, I was all signed up for my classes and feeling excited about where the future would take me. Little did I know, that summer, my life would change forever. I would meet my future wife who was a senior in high school and ultimately ended up attending the same college as I did, just one year behind. She, too, majored in psychology. As we moved through the first few years, my career aspirations didn't change, but hers did. She eventually decided that she wanted to practice law. She ended up graduating and moved on to law school. When she made the determination to practice law, my perspective changed a little. I knew that once she graduated law school, she would have to take the bar exam in whichever state we lived in. I knew, with the mobility agreement, the FBI would require that I couldn't subject her to the whims of moving around from state to state. I reconciled with this realization and determined that I would still pursue a career in law enforcement as a police officer. After I graduated from college, I applied to various police departments. Finally, after a year or two, my current department called me back. I went through the interview process and was eventually offered a job. I had a difficult decision to make. I could leave the sleepy suburb of Buffalo (Lancaster, NY) and all my family behind and start the career I always wanted, or I could wait in Buffalo in hopes that I would make my way up the hiring list and be hired by one of the local agencies. I decided (along with my brother) to take the job opportunity. Here we were, two brothers from the hills of New York, about to move to the metropolitan area of the nation's capital and become police officers.

There was a stark difference between the way of life from Lancaster, NY, and the way of life in a big city. Being a skinny, college kid from a private school, with all academic achievements and little athletic achievements I heard nonstop about how I was book smart but not "street smart." As I progressed through the police academy, I tried to reconcile the two. I started to wonder, could you be both? Can you be book smart and still be "street smart" even though you didn't grow up in the city? As I went through the academy, I maintained the title of the "smart guy" but still heard the same drumbeat about "street smarts" and how they will get you further in this career.

After I graduated and started to patrol, I was timid at first. Not only was police work a new experience for me but so to was being in a big city. The first few months of my career, I did what I knew to do. I stayed back a little, observed, and assessed. At about the fourth month or so, I started to realize that you didn't have to choose between being book smart and "street smart"; you could be both. I realized that many of the skills that allowed me to achieve academic success could be used to develop "street smart" skills. I started to realize that my years of studying profiling books, psychology, sociology, and forensic psychology had allowed me to understand motivations of people, and if you can understand motivations of people, you can start to predict behavior patterns. I started to watch people more. I started to read body language indicators. I started to use my verbal skills and powers of perception during my stops. I started to talk to my wife and learn how lawyers think, how they react, how they design questioning and trial strategies against police officers. I started to pick up legal books and books written by lawyers and learn their cross-examination techniques and argument styles. It helped me two-fold; not only did I learn how lawyers would question me, but I also learned how to formulate counter arguments. Learning this argument style has helped me on patrol, in the stationhouse, and in the courtroom. All of a sudden, everything clicked, and I exploded. I was stopping people at a frenzied pace. I became good friends with other officers that had similar outlooks and experiences. I noticed that as time went on, my arrests were getting better and better. I started to read behavioral indicators so well that it almost got boring. I could almost predict their physical reactions and verbal responses. This allowed me to be several steps ahead of them. I slowly started to realize that I could strategize before stops. I realized that I could conceptualize the stop in my head. That by doing this, I could prevent mistakes and execute stops in such a manner that they would be airtight for prosecution. I started to learn the in-and-outs of the job. I started to get experience with different types of arrests and different types of courts. It helped mold me into a better police officer. I started to develop that police instinct. He is that little guy on my shoulder that I always listen to not only for sound advice but also for sound judgment.

I'm not saying this to make myself sound good. I am saying this so that after you read this book, you too can do the same things. My hope is that by reading this book, you too can speed your learning curve up. You need not make the mistakes that I did, but you can enjoy the spoils of learning through my mistakes instead of making them yourself.

The title of this book comes from a term my close friends and I used to describe the officer we are always seeking to become. A "rookie" is an officer who is new, fresh out of the academy to a few years in, still learning the basics. A "veteran" is an officer who has simply been doing the job for a while. Most departments define an officer who has been a police officer for over five years to be a "veteran." But your goal should not be to simply become a veteran. The tubby doughnut-munching school resource officer who has only made a handful of arrests his entire twenty-year career is a veteran. The word "veteran" may sound impressive to the media or carry with it some expectation of competence, but we all know that time on isn't necessarily commensurate with experience. Police officers like you and I seek something more than "veteran" status. We want to be proven. We want to go home at the end of every shift, look ourselves in the mirror, and be proud of what we accomplished that day, whether it was taking a bad guy off the street or talking down a suicidal subject. The proven officer is the one who has intentionally made his life difficult by involving himself in uncomfortable and difficult patrol situations, and then on top of that, has made a mess of those situations, as you will see that I have, but then who has the presence of mind to assess, learn and decide "I'll never let that happen again." The proven officer is the one who doesn't see police work as a paycheck and benefits package, but rather has a genuine contempt for evil men and enjoys beating them at their own game. The proven officer is not a superhero. He gets tired, stressed, scared, and disgusted. He hobbles out of bed in the morning with aches and pains. He drags himself to the gym to work out. He drags himself to court in the morning after working a late arrest the night before. Why? Because he has to. Because no one else is willing to dip their hands in the filth so that others may live in peace. Because he has taken an oath and has committed his life to the betterment of society. The proven officer, unlike the mere veteran, continues to seek out these difficult experiences because he knows that smooth seas do not make good sailors. The proven officer has already been involved in any situation he will come across at least once, because he made it his business to involve himself in those situations the first time. Reading this book will not make you a proven officer . . . that only comes with hard work and experience. The point of this book is to expose you to my particular road to becoming a proven officer and all that I've learned along the way, mostly from my own mistakes, so that you will have the confidence to get out there and make yourself a proven officer and know that your road to that status is just as rocky as everyone else's. And that's the point.

As you read through this book, you will notice what it's missing. You will notice that there aren't very many references or footnotes. That, simply put, is because I didn't use very many to create this book. The reference material for the preceding pages mostly lies in the experience that I have gained from thousands of person stops and thousands more consensual encounters, interactions, and vehicle stops that I've made over my career. Perhaps one of the questions that I get asked most frequently is, how? How did you learn to talk to people like that? How did you get those drugs off that individual? How did you notice that person doing that? The answer I always give is the same. I learned all those things from doing the job. I learned those things from making the stops. My experiences have been forged through countless stops, each one allowing me to learn and refine my craft. I learned those things from not being afraid of failure, from jumping into situations, and learning from my successes and more importantly from my mistakes. You, too, can learn this way. You have to be committed to doing the job you signed up to do. The only thing that is preventing you is the will power. Don't be afraid of failure. We all fail, and we all make mistakes. The most successful of us learn from those mistakes and move on to be that much smarter for the next stop. Criminals thrive on the weak. They thrive on those that can be manipulated and that are indecisive. Don't be that officer. Learn to do the job, make the stops, and you too will be a force for good. You, too, will develop a reputation for excellence. And you, too, will have earned the right to wear the badge on your chest and represent, to the best of your ability, those that have sacrificed their lives for that same badge. Honor the memory of the fallen. Honor the oath that you took. Honor them by setting out and achieving what you all signed up to do.

This book is designed for mostly new police officers. Officers with less than a few years on the job, but I would be remise if I didn't say that I'm confident that any police officer could learn something from these pages. We all know that time on isn't necessarily commensurate with experience.

I hope you enjoy reading this book, but more importantly, I hope that you learn something. I hope the material in these pages helps you to become a better police officer. A police officer that is well rounded and multifaceted. Now let's go.

PART

One

CHAPTER

1

This job is like no other in the world. The amount of material we are expected to know is both endless and ever changing. The stakes are always high, and we will never know what the next minute will bring. It's important to prepare yourself physically, mentally, and emotionally for the career in which you are about to embark on.

Prepare Yourself Physically

Don't be the police officer that always bears the brunt of the doughnut jokes. Make sure you take care of your body physically. Get a proper diet plan in place. Make sure you're working out and training regularly. Remember any person that you pass on patrol no matter the size you might have to fight. I've arrested guys as small as 80 pounds and as large as 370 pounds. You never know when you will have to be ready to take action. You need to prepare yourself physically. It's easy to let physical training get away from you because of the time constraints this job will bring on your personal life; however, with the amount of tools and information available today, there really aren't many excuses as to why you can't fit a few minutes of physical training in a day.

Speaking of preparing yourself physically, make sure you get your sleep in. If possible, try and get a sleep routine down. This job is unpredictable, and you will learn to get by on little to no sleep. You still need to do your best and make sure your sleep is consistent as possible whenever possible so you can maintain a certain functioning level. You are no good to anybody if you can't perform because of lack of sleep. In a job where decision-making and reaction time are crucial, make sure you are doing what you can to get the sleep you need.

Keep up on your training. As police officers, we can never get enough training. It is your job to make sure that you keep up with the different kinds of training that is available to you. If possible, try and vary the training so you can get a little bit of everything in. Defensive tactics, legal, firearms, etc., they're all important. Obtain the legal codes in the jurisdictions you patrol and review selected codes every now and then. When you're bored, grab the traffic code and check out a few new statues. Carry around pocket guides of the local codes for quick reference. Expanding your knowledge base will add value you can only dream of. Many officers will create "cheat sheets" of codes that they frequently use for quick access. Make sure that you keep up with changes in case law in your area. Case law is always changing and is often different from state to state. It's important to be as up to date as possible so you are making the best decision possible when it comes to being in compliance with the most recent changes to the law.

Video Training

Real-time training is hard to come by in this profession, don't be afraid to go online and check out some videos of police encounters and shootings. See how the officers in those situations reacted. Learn from their successes and mistakes. Put yourself in their shoes and try to determine what you would have done. Be the backup quarterback on the sidelines running mental reps through his head so when his number is called he can fluidly step in and perform at a high level. Look at the body language indicators on those videos. Once you watch enough, you will start to become an expert at telegraphing suspect behavior. Use that knowledge and apply it to your stops. There are too many scenarios that we can be subjected to. It will take too much time and is not even be possible to be exposed to all the possible scenarios that we might encounter. That's why it's important that we learn from each other. We can speed up the learning curve by training in this manner.

Sharpshooter

Don't neglect your firearms training. Many departments only have either annual or semi-annual training with your firearm. That is not enough. Try and find time to practice on your own. Just because you're not practicing doesn't mean the criminal is also not practicing. In an FBI interview of convicted cop killers, some offenders stated that they practice many times a week because they were under the impression that police "go to the range two, three times a week, practice arms so they can hit anything"[1]. If criminals are at the range practicing so should you be at the range practicing. And while you are there, get creative. Look for other courses that involve more than static shooting. Go outside your comfort zone because that's where the real learning takes place.

Prepare Yourself Mentally

You will hear often that you need to have the "warriors" mind-set. While this book is not intended to be a guide on that topic, it's absolutely true. I want to share with you a story of a

---

[1] Darrin Weiner. FBI Findings on Cop Killers. Posted April 04, 2013. Accessed April 18, 2016. www.Calgunlaws.com/fbi-finds-on-cop-killers/

situation that I encountered that really put this job in perspective for me.

I was on foot patrol. I was solo, and it was around ten thirty at night on a weekend. I was in an area where PCP use had just started to spike. I received a radio run for a "sick" person that was lying on a small berm. As I approached the individual, I could see that his personal property was strewn about. He was sitting on the ground and rocking in the fetal position. He wasn't a large man at about 5'9' and 180 pounds. I immediately realized he was not "sick" but was under the influence of PCP. One of the factors that you need to take into account when dealing with individuals that are under the influence of PCP is that they are often impervious to pain. I immediately called for additional units. As he noticed me, he brought his head up from between his knees and asked if I was there to kill him. Before I could respond, he charged at me. It was very quick, and I didn't have time to pull out any of my nonlethal weapons. As he made contact with me, I was able to kind of hip toss him into some steel newspaper boxes. As he went crashing through about six newspaper boxes, I figured that would be enough, and he would be down for the count. Much to my chagrin, he sprung up like a jack-in-the-box and continued to engage me. We traded several blows and continued to grapple while standing. Realizing it was hopeless to continue to box this guy, I was able to take him to the ground. The entire time my radio was out of range, and I was unable to put any additional information out to dispatch. I would later learn that dispatch had sent my backup to the wrong area of town nowhere close to where I was. As we continued to fight on the ground, I started to wonder how long I could continue to fight for. I had already been fighting for several minutes to no avail. I started to think in my head about whether I would have to use lethal force against this individual if I reached the point of exhaustion.

At that moment, my lungs were on fire, and I had multiple cuts and bruises. Time kind of stood real still, and I started to picture my wife, son, and family in my mind. I started to realize that if I lost tonight, I could lose everything. I made the determination that I would not lose on that night. Just then, my body experienced the biggest adrenaline dump I have ever received. I was able to flip the individual over and get him into rear, back-to-belly control technique.

As I continued to lock the move into place, I could smell the PCP heavy on the individual's body. His head was rubbing against my face, and I could smell his stench permeating from his body. I could feel his arms clutching and clawing at mine, and I could feel him moving his head down in an effort to bite my arm. As I continued to lock the hold in place, I could start to hear a sickening tearing sound that anyone that has played sports recognizes. Just then, I felt the sensation of the MCL in my right elbow reaching its limits and slowly tearing. I powered through the pain and locked the move in enough to feel the individual go slightly limp. Just then, while maintaining my position, I reached around and was able to pull my handcuffs out and handcuff his hands in the front of his body. This reenergized him, and he continued to try and attempt to head butt me. Just then, I saw blue flashing lights whizzing in. The backup units arrived and pulled the individual away from my grasp just as I blacked out from exertion.

I only remained that way for about thirty seconds or so, then I was able to regain my bearings. It took thirteen officers, two stun guns, and three pairs of handcuffs to subdue the individual. It turns out that dispatch had attempted to disregard my backup because they didn't think I required additional assistance with a "sick" person. When they realized they had mistaken me with another officer, they sent my backup to another location. I don't know how long I took, but I ended up fighting this guy for about five to seven minutes. Anyone familiar with that level of exertion knows that normal humans can fight at maximum exertion for about thirty to forty-five seconds uninterrupted. Athletes can probably fight at all out exertion for forty-five to seventy-five seconds.

I'm not sharing this story with you to make myself seem like some kind of tough guy. I'm sharing this story with you to show you the real emotions and thoughts you will experience during stressful situations like that. In the heat of the moment, you will face adversity, you will be hit, and it's up to you to determine how you will handle it. You have to power through the injuries, bumps, and bruises and decide right then and there that you will win. You will do whatever necessary to make sure that you make it through the encounter safely. You will experience emotions, and that's all right. They will be some of the most powerful motivators that you could ever hope for. It's okay to be nervous. It's the manner in which we respond to those nerves that will define us and allow us to persevere through hardships.

Learn to control your emotions. We deal with a lot of high-stress situations. There comes a time after the incident calms down where we, too, need to reel in our emotions. Don't let yourself get carried away and do something that you'll regret. In terms of force, remember to only use that in which is necessary and nothing more. When the handcuffs are on, it is over. And when it's over, it's over. It's not worth losing your cool and losing your job. If you need to walk away, let another officer know and walk away to calm down. There is no shame in needing to temporarily disconnect yourself from a scene, after it is safe, in order to dial yourself in and make sure you remain composed. Don't let suspects bait you. Don't let other citizens bait you. Most police naysayers are looking for some kind of reaction from you that they can use to their advantage. Don't give it to them. Maintain your composure and present yourself in a calm, professional, and businesslike manner.

Prepare Your Partner

Typically police officers will gravitate around other officers that share similar police styles as they do. Selecting and working closely with a group of individuals that you can trust will not only help you grow as an officer but will also allow you to have a peace of mind. That peace of mind comes from the fact that you can trust those officers to watch your back. You need not worry about anything other than the person in front of you because a trusted partner will take care of the rest. You need to find a partner that you can trust with your life. You need a partner that can finish your sentences for you. You need a partner that can know what you're thinking without being told. You need a partner that you can seamlessly move in and out of a stop with. You need someone that knows and compliments your style. You also need a partner that you can learn from. Each of you has to contribute to the team in order for the team to be successful. There is no greater peace of mind than when you isolate that group of individuals that you can trust and work with. Selecting a good partner will enable you to live up to your full potential as a police officer. They will drive, motivate, and you will encourage each other to be the best you can be. But most of all, they will ensure that you remain safe. They'll ensure that they will move heaven and earth to make sure that you both return home alive and in the same condition as you left.

CHAPTER

2

Managing Your Ego

You're gearing up for your first day on the job. You look in the mirror and your uniform looks good, you check to make sure all your equipment is in your bag and in working order, you grab your lunch, and you're out the door. You're hoping you didn't forget anything, but there is one thing that you should've left behind—your ego. Your ego really has no place in the police setting. Now I don't want you to confuse the difference between confidence and ego because we will need confidence. The difference is that confident people know when they need to tone their ego down. In this job, the first thing that will get you into trouble will be your ego. I often say that our egos will get us fired or jailed and for good reason. If you look at the majority of the negative videos or articles portraying police, it'll almost always center on some sort of ego issue that most likely could have been avoided in the first place.

The first thing that will allow the public to turn against us is our own ego and how we portray it. How many times have you heard, "Oh, just because you're a cop, you think you're better than everyone else?" If you haven't heard it yet, you will at some point. While this attitude may be unfair, sometimes perception is reality. We need to remember while we are out on patrol to keep the big picture in sight. The big picture is that we all represent the profession and integrity of the badge. Every one of us regardless of the jurisdiction, geographical locations,

PROVEN   15

or unit represents every other police officer in the world. Don't give the police naysayers the ammunition they need to perpetuate a negative stereotype of police by letting your ego get into your decision making. The police naysayers are just waiting for us to mess up so they can cry foul. Let's show them that we are one step ahead of them. That we will carry ourselves with professionalism and decorum at all times. Let's rob them of the argument that police are corrupt, egotistical maniacs and instead remind them that we are guided by strong values and morals, and we will always act in an ethical and legal way when conducting our jobs. Letting our egos get involved into our decision-making lets the ugly beast of police naysayers out of Pandora's box where they will wreak havoc on the profession that we hold so dear. I want to explore a few areas in which your ego could corrupt your decision-making, leading to poor decision-making and a negative perception of police.

Smile, You're on Camera

Here in the twenty-first century, police officers have to deal with a stark reality that many of our predecessors did not. That is the introduction of the video age. Especially in today's media culture, our actions can be broadcasted almost instantaneously. Cellphone cameras enable almost instant dissemination of video footage. Almost all the footage is mostly unedited and without context. Oftentimes, individuals will start taping midway through the stop and their video will lack context and most certainly will portray the police in as negative a way as possible. Is it unfair; yes, it is. Is there much we can do about it? Yes, there is.

Instead of getting into an argument with the person taping only to predictably be shouted at by the videographer, "It's my right, man!" just simply ignore the person. As long as they are at a safe distance, not interfering with your crime scene or investigation, and in a place that they are legally entitled to be in, there's really nothing you can do about it. You stand to be embarrassed, and you will fall right into the trap of the person taping if you attempt to intervene with the person taping you. This is, of course, the exact behavior they want, and it will turn a normal scene into a chaotic one very quickly. Don't let your ego get in a tug-of-war with the person over their cellphone.

In addition to making you look bad, there can be civil, administrative, and/or criminal penalties for taking someone's property from them when there is no probable cause to do so. Many officers will get so infatuated with the camera that they start to compromise officer safety during the stop. The person that poses the most threat to you is the person that you have stopped in front of you, not some bored, activist passerby with nothing else to do. If you are being videotaped, use it as an opportunity to let the videographer capture nothing more than the pristine example of a professional police officer. When you let the videographer impact the way in which you run your stops, then you will make mistakes. Instead don't stray from the way in which you normally conduct business. The only thing you want the videographer leaving the scene with is a video that will bore them, use up additional storage on their phone, and be used as a training video for police on how to conduct the perfect stop. Remember, in the twenty-first century, we are most likely being video- and audio-recorded for most of our interactions with the public anyway. One more camera that you actually know is taping you won't make a difference. Remain poised and don't let your ego give the police naysayers what they want.

Am I Free to Go?

Another area that I will frequently see an officer's ego get in the way is during encounters with individuals. Remember, the difference between a stop and a consensual encounter is that during a stop, the person is not free to go. Egos can negatively impact this differentiation. I have seen a lot of officers attempt to stop or seize someone that is otherwise free to go because they think that they have to flex their muscles and show the other person who the boss is. They think they need to demand respect from the individual. This is a sure way to get you into trouble. If a person is free to go, meaning you have no reasonable suspicion to stop them and no probable cause to arrest them, then they are free to go. Don't let your ego take it personally. You serve only one group's interests by making an illegal stop and subsequent seizure or arrest, and that is the police naysayers. By acting in this manner, you will once again perpetuate the myth that police are out illegally stopping people. If the person you have before you expresses that they wish to leave, let them leave (if they are free to do so). Many officers will get flustered when individuals ask them, "Am I free to go?" Don't be. If they are free to go, say yes; if they aren't free to go, say no. Don't take the statement personally, especially if they're free to go. Even if you suspect they might be guilty but you have nothing to go on, live to fight another day. All criminals will be caught at some time or another. Let the individual consider himself or herself lucky that day. Move onto the next stop because, trust me, there will be many more. Don't let your ego prevent you from releasing individuals that are free to go. It's not worth it.

If You're Wrong, You're Wrong

When you're wrong, you're wrong, and don't let your ego tell you differently. A lot of times, we tend to go down this path of "we are right and you are wrong" even when the evidence is against us. It doesn't have to be that way. Don't let your ego drag you down that path.

Remember, you can always stop when you discover you have made a mistake and take the proper remedies. If you find yourself going down that path, stop and take a few minutes to reassess the evidence. We are an evidence-based profession and that means that we have to follow the evidence even when it falls against us. This often occurs when we discover there is some kind of discrepancy in the law we are trying to enforce. If we are confronted with evidence that the person we stopped didn't commit whatever we have accused them of committing, no problem.

Take a few steps back, review the information, and make the most informed decision you can. Don't give the police naysayers any additional ammunition because your ego couldn't handle being wrong. If you pull someone over and tell them they ran a stop sign, and if turns out it was a yield sign, don't continue to lecture the person and find some other charge. Own your mistake, do the right thing, and move on unscathed.

I've had many scenarios where I thought someone did something they didn't or possessed something that turned out to be nothing. You'll make similar mistakes. Instead of letting your ego weasel into the decision-making process and dooming you down the path of no return, simply stop, reassess, and make the appropriate decision. The high road is the tough road most of the time, but it is the right road. There is no shame in fessing up when you made a mistake. It may be embarrassing, but believe me, the alternative will not only be embarrassing, but it will be damaging. When you're beat, you're beat. Even the best athletes get beat. Nobody knows everything or wins 100 percent of the time. Focus on the big picture, the integrity of the profession.

This Is My . . .

How many times have you seen a video where the police officer professes ownership over something that he clearly doesn't own? It will sound something like, "This is my road, building, station, sidewalk etc." Don't get caught up in that word game. As we've been discussing, your ego can lead you to say and do a lot of things that will be damaging to yourself and the profession. Statements like this will only lead to infuriate the person that is receiving these statements and will perpetuate the myth of police officers as egotistical maniacs that don't care for the public and only got the job so they can boss people around. Don't fall into that category by saying something dumb like that. We'll talk a lot about how to talk to people in the later chapters and that example is example number 1 of what not to say. Remember what your mom said, manners would get you a lot farther along than rudeness. This also goes for police work. We are under the microscope 24-7. Let's not let our egos get the best of us. Instead, let's put our best foot forward.

You're Still Talking?

There will certainly come a time where you are confronted with an individual that is being rude, dismissive, and vociferous. If they aren't stopped or they haven't committed a criminal offense for which you can stop them for, you are best served by ignoring them and walking or driving away. Many police officers let their egos get the better of them when confronted with these situations. It is important to remember that we, as Americans, enjoy the protections of the First Amendment of the US Constitution, which includes the protection for free speech. Generally speaking, as long as the speech isn't inciting violence, creating an unsafe environment, or violating a statue (such as disorderly conduct), the individual is free to say as they please. Much of the language will be disrespectful or hurtful to you, but it is still free speech nonetheless. We as police officers are expected to have big shoulders and tough skin and not allow incendiary language like that affect us. If you are confronted with an individual that is trying to engage you in a dialogue based on incendiary language, simply ignore them and walk away. Don't fall into their trap. Don't respond. Don't engage them in conversation if it isn't necessary. Don't approach them. Don't search the codebook and stretch their behavior into some kind of criminal or civil charge. Manage your ego, remember the big picture, and walk away. You don't need to be on video or receive a complaint because your ego couldn't handle some heckler.

You Want to Complain about Me?

When it comes to citizen complaints, it's very easy to let our egos really damage the interaction. Many officers will get flustered when they hear a citizen say they wish to complain or that they wish to have the officer's name and/or badge number. Don't get flustered and don't let your ego take control. Fight the urge to say some snide comment, withhold the information, or argue with the person. Whatever your general orders or SOPs require that you provide to the citizen, just provide it.

After you provide it, if possible, simply walk away. Don't stick around and engage in some prolonged argument that will lead nowhere. Fight your ego's urge to engage and instead disengage. The last thing you need to do is get so irate that the individual wants to complain that you acted out of order. Trust me, I've been there. I know how enraged you can get when you are just trying to do your job and someone has the audacity to levy charges of impropriety against you or someone wants to tell you how to do your job. It makes all of us angry, but remember the big picture and don't let your ego get in the way and further damage the interaction.

In situations where I believe a complaint is forthcoming, I will take some time to make some detailed notes. Treat it almost like writing an arrest narrative. I will include the facts of the encounter and any quotes by either party. I always want the most precise recollection of the events to be mine. That way, I have some evidence to counter exaggerated claims. Depending on your working relationship with your supervisors, it might even be prudent to contact them just to give them a heads up about the event. This will allow them to hear your version of events first before the other person's version and will help them determine the best course of action to take.

Keeping your ego out of your police work will serve you well during your career. There are a lot of naysayers that are out to portray the police in the least favorable light as possible. Don't give them the opportunity.

CHAPTER

3

Nice Guys Finish Last

It's difficult for a lot of new police officers to reconcile with the fact that people will no longer initially judge them on the merits of their character, but they will judge them based on the merits that they are a police officer. When dealing with criminals, there is a stark distinction that needs to be drawn between being nice and conducting your job in a safe manner. While it is important to conduct yourself in a polite and courteous manner, that needs to be turned off at a moment's notice if need be.

Human beings have a nature inclination to want to be nice to each other. We typically are socialized from an early age to be nice to others and to avoid conflict with others. This stems from an innate desire for self-preservation. The more conflict early humans engaged in the more likely they were to be injured or killed. Keeping in mind that to early humans, even the smallest of injuries could be fatal. Due to the career we have chosen, sometimes those things are not possible. Sometimes conflict might find us, and we need not be nice any longer. It is difficult for a new police officer to learn to temper that niceness, but it must be done.

We see this behavior most often interfere with the ability to stop and take enforcement action against an individual. Most new officers can stop the person but will feel bad taking further action like arresting the individual or citing them. Remember, it's their behavior that has led to your interaction with them. They own the responsibility for the corrective action taken against them, not you. I will often tell my new trainees that your discretion should be somewhat limited for the first six to twelve months. This is not to say that you can't use discretion; however, you need to make sure that you can break that natural inclination to be nice and let people walk away without facing the consequences of their actions.

The only way to learn the job is to make the stops. Letting people off, especially early in your career because you are trying to be nice, is the easy way out and will hurt you in your ability to develop your police instinct. It's always easier to appear to be the "good" cop and allow the person off with a "verbal warning." It's much tougher to be the "bad" cop and take enforcement action against that person. It sounds harsh, but in order to learn how to stop people and be successful as a police officer, you need to be able to break down that "niceness" barrier. Once you have broken it down and realize that you have the ability to stop anyone for anything, then you can start to bring more discretion into your decision-making. It's similar to what the military does in boot camp. You need to break down those barriers so you can rebuild them with your new career in mind.

As we get further into the book, you will hear me talk a lot about disarming your suspect with language and compassion. I don't want you to mistake this behavior for being "nice."

The context in which I refer to being nice and using compassion applies to a strategy that you can employ to either extract information from the individual or make the scene safer by disarming an aggressive or non-compliant individual using language skills. These are conducted through verbal strategies designed to disarm the suspect not yourself. You will see a lot of officers start to disarm themselves by using language that is sympathetic to the suspect that they have stopped. They'll erroneously try to develop a rapport with the individual and identify with them by mimicking their speech patterns. They think if they connect with and personalize themselves with the suspect that the suspect will have more respect for them. This notion is false. Behavior like that will almost always backfire. The suspect is more likely to interpret behavior like that as an opportunity for them to gain the upper hand on you. They may hear language like that and equate it to weakness. If this happens, rest assured they will attempt to wrestle control of the scene from you. This will lead to them being combative (verbally or physically), dismissive of your authority, and make it more likely that the stop will end poorly.

We will discuss later on the importance of learning to talk to suspects and developing a rapport with them. The information we just covered in the previous section is not the appropriate way to go about that.

In 1992, the FBI released a study named "Killed in the Line of Duty." The authors of the study interviewed fifty individuals that were convicted of murdering police officers. The study was then used to develop a number of traits that victim officers exhibited. Many of these traits are attributed to what I term as being "nice." Most of the victim officers were termed by their colleagues as "well liked," "laid back," and easygoing.[2] On their face, these behaviors might not sound bad, but overly friendly behavior can backfire on you. Being overly friendly to the suspect can lead to you developing a sense of complacency. You'll see this complacency lead to officers to be almost incredulous when suspects assault them. This complacency can lead

<hr>

[2] Chuck Remsburg. Traits That Get Cops Killed. Accessed April 18, 2016. http://www.poam.net/train-and-educate/2008/train-educate/

to officers not understanding that people will lie to them. They'll get complacent and start to believe that everyone is as nice to them and that other individuals are not capable of nefarious behavior. This complacency will lead to adverse situations because their "niceness" will have disarmed themselves.

Another subset of this occurs during stops and subsequent arrests. You'll see officers that are overly friendly and oftentimes grant "favors" to the suspect. A great many individuals that we will stop are not stupid and will learn how to manipulate those that can be manipulated. Suspects will know that in order to execute whatever plan they are cooking up in their head, they need an officer that will be friendly and sympathetic to them. I have seen many officers be "nice" by allowing suspects to answer phones during stops. Not wanting to appear "mean," they grant them special favors thinking it will grant them some kind of "street cred capital" with the suspect. How do you know that as the suspect is reaching into his pocket, he didn't just concoct that story to give him an excuse to retrieve his weapon and shoot you? You don't. One of the other traits of slain officers was that they were more prone to shortcut procedures or rules.[2] This goes hand in hand with the favors part because most often, to grant favors, you need to sidestep the rules.

In regards to post-arrest procedures, this is an area where you will see many officers skirt the rules in the name of being friendly. This includes behavior such as loosening the handcuffs because they are "too tight." We have all been trained on how to handcuff someone. If you test the handcuffs and they are indeed too tight, take appropriate safety precautions and adjust them accordingly. Do not adjust them blindly just because you are trying to placate to your arrestee. When searching individuals, don't lay prey to the "niceness" trap and cut corners. The last thing you need to do is to allow a suspect to retain a weapon because you were trying to "cut them a break" by hastily searching them.

Procedures for transporting are often skirted in the name of "niceness." Things like not seat belting your suspect because they say it makes them uncomfortable or perhaps it will make it less noticeable to you when they retrieve a weapon. Things like handcuffing from the front because he's not a violent offender can get you into trouble. You will see that the more interactions an officer has with a suspect, the more likely they are to grant them favors because they "know" them. Don't get caught in that trap. Like I said before, suspects will use any opportunity to manipulate a situation. You're being nice by following procedural guidelines and acting in a respectful manner.

In today's society, there has been this push to make police officer's more "service orientated." While it sounds good for chiefs and politicians to say at news conferences, I think they have misunderstood the difference between having an attitude of customer service and having an attitude that imparts dignity and respect to individual, however, still allows you to maintain a culture of safety. Another one of the traits of slain officer was that the "tends to perceive self as more public relations than law enforcement"[3]. This attitude creates conflicting messages for police officers. On one hand, you can have the chief or your supervisors hammering home that you need to be "customer service" oriented. That customer-service mentality has particular traits that are associated with it that may not be conducive to creating a safe environment.

---

[3] Chuck Remsburg. Traits That Get Cops Killed. Accessed April 18, 2016. http://www.poam.net/train-and-educate/2008/train-educate/

In our career, the customer is not always right and belief in that could lead to dangerous consequences. We can't treat certain circumstances like a food service manager trying to go out of our way to placate an angry customer. It just doesn't work that way. Sometimes, we have to have it our way, not the other way around. Don't fall into that trap. This isn't to say that you can't use courtesy and respect when necessary. It just means you need to be able to flip the switch the other way if your scene starts to get out of your control. In today's society, the message we're receiving from politicians and some chiefs make it difficult for some officers to be able to transition out of that customer-service mentality.

I was at a training class one time, and we were discussing rapid interviewing techniques of individuals that we had stopped. The instructor lead with the premise of we should always assume the person we have stopped is lying to us. Now many people think that is harsh or unfair, but in the police world, that statement is true. One of the officers in the class raised his hand and said he would have a hard time implementing that mind-set. He believed that man was inherently nice and incapable of lying at that capacity. I told him what I tell most of my new officers. If you have a tough time coming to grips with the fact that most individuals we come in contact with will lie at some point in the interaction, start with a neutral premises and let that person prove to you why what they're saying is truthful. We're an evidence-based profession so let them present evidence to you as to why what they're saying is true. If they can't provide the evidence, well then, they most likely shouldn't be believed.

This brings me to my next point. It is the final trait of slain officers that the FBI study revealed. The victim officers were too often too "trusting" of their ability to "read" the persons internal motivations.[4] Remember, we read external behavioral patterns, not internal motivations. These officers tended to look for the "good" in people. They were most often classified as optimists and were often susceptible to believing offenders claims of cooperation. I don't want this to come of the wrong way because there are billions of decent people on the face of this earth. However, when you are in this career, you can't afford to have a blanket optimism view of the world.

I'm sorry to say it just doesn't happen that way. There are people out there that are capable of violence and despicable acts. There are people out there that will perceive kindness for weakness. And there are people out there that will manipulate those that are naïve to the fact that evil exists. When the badge is on your chest, you need to be a little more skeptical about what others are capable of. You need to realize that evil does exist and you need to prepare yourself for it. You can still maintain a positive outlook on life and have a happy-go-lucky attitude. However, you will need to learn to control it and when it will be necessary to turn it off completely.

Don't get sucked into the nice trap. Don't disarm yourself with your own "niceness" or naivety. You can be respectful and treat others with dignity while at the same time maintaining the level of vigilance that this career demands.

[4] Chuck Remsburg. Traits That Get Cops Killed. Accessed April 18, 2016. http://www.poam.net/train-and-educate/2008/train-educate/

C H A P T E R

4

Controlling Your Suspect

Law enforcement is a career where certain skills are critical. The absence of these particular skills will have dire consequences. One of these skills is the ability to control the individual you have stopped. This oftentimes is one of the most difficult skills that new officers have to master. While it is possible to have experience with this skill in previous careers such as the military, it's a skill that most individuals will not have had much experience with. The importance of this skill can't be underscored. The failure to control your suspect during a stop could lead to serious injury or death. We have seen and heard too many stories of officers being killed in the line of duty only afterward to hear that the suspect took control of the scene.

In the study "Killed in the Line of Duty.", the authors interviewed fifty individuals that were convicted of murdering police officers. The objective of the study was to gain insight into the mind of the killers and determine why and how they choose to murder their police officer victims. After you review their findings, there is one thing sticks out. The offenders for the most part commented that they killed the police officers because they had some sort of opportunity to do so. Either the police officer was too distracted doing some other function related to the stop such as working the radio to pay attention to them or the police officer had failed to control the suspect. During the course of the stop, the offender was allowed to reach into their pockets or turn away from the police officer without recourse. One offender even states, "He did not take control of me, He never controlled my actions successfully." The offender was able to turn away from the police officer, retrieve a gun, and then he turned around and shot the police officer, murdering him.[5]

I don't mention this study to use scare tactics. I mention this study to once again highlight the importance of controlling your individual during the stop. Many new officers are timid to begin with. Stopping and controlling people is a new experience and requires time to master. In order to master the skill of controlling your individual, you need to start stopping people.

Who's the Boss?

As you are stopping individuals, remember that you're the boss. This is not to say that you should let your ego take over and be rude and dismissive to the individual. This is to say that you need to be firm and establish control early. Most times, just the fact that we're police officers will exude enough authority over the individual to control them without any further action. However, if the individual you have stopped has nefarious intentions or is familiar with police interactions, they may challenge you in an effort to see just how much leeway they have. Just as we're stopping and sizing up individuals, so too is the person that we're stopping sizing us up. They'll make quick judgments regarding our level of physical fitness, our attentiveness to them, and our overall acumen as police officers.

[5] Francis Clines. Police Killers Offer Insights into Victim's Fatal Mistakes. Posted March 9, 1993. Accessed April 18, 2016.
http://nytimes.com/1993/03/09/us/police-killers-offer-insights-into-victims-fatal-mistakes.html

We hear all the time about the importance of good command presence. Good command presence can be the first rung in the ladder that leads to controlling your individual successfully. Included in command presence is your general appearance. Make sure that your uniform is well kept and exudes authority. Shine what needs to be shined and make any necessary repairs. Make sure your equipment is in working order and inspect it for obvious signs of wear. The last thing you need is for the suspect you have stopped to notice how rusty your handcuffs are. This will indicate to them that you never use them and could encourage them to become more defiant. While that's an obvious example, the suspect will look for any signs that indicate that you are lazy or incompetent because they then know they can control the scene. When you approach the individual and start to engage them in conversation, make sure you use a firm voice and keep your volume to an appropriate level that will allow them to hear you but also exudes authority. As you are speaking with them, make eye contact and pay attention to their movements. Establish control from the first moment. This will set the tone for the stop and send a message to the individuals that anything other than compliance will not be tolerated. Direct the individual to an area that is advantageous to you. Immediately make it clear that furtive gestures or motions in and out of their pockets will not be tolerated. Make sure their hands are visible at all times.

I have seen many officers allow the individual to keep their hands behind their backs while they are speaking with them. While the most common place for an individual to conceal a handgun is in the front of their waistband, the small of the back comes in second. We will talk at length about recognizing body language and behavioral indicators later in the book. Behavioral indicators and body language are important to pay attention to because they allow us to read clues that might telegraph an individual's next act, thus buying us more time to react to them. These indicators are useless if you ignore or don't act on them. As we get further into the book, you will begin to learn the signs that you will need to be aware of.

When we talk about reading body language and behavioral indicators, many people mistake these with "reading people." The ability to "read people" refers to the fact that we are attempting to read internal psychological motivations through outward actions. That we are interested in the "why" part of whatever action is taking place inside of the suspect's head. This is a falsehood. As police officers, we really don't need to be concerned at that moment why they might do something only that they could do something. This is where reading their behavioral indicators and body language will come into play. If the person you have stopped in exhibiting any of these behavior indicators, take control of them immediately.

Keep It Simple, Ask, Tell, Make

You can do this either through verbal commands or physical actions. When using verbal commands, be firm and direct with what you want the individual to do. Keep your commands short and simple. Ensure that the individual complies with whatever you have said and don't get into the habit of repeating yourself more than twice before taking action. If a suspect keeps placing his hands in his pockets after being told once or twice, don't continue to allow them to engage in this behavior. Formulate your reasonable suspicion and conduct a Terry pat down immediately. You simply cannot afford to let your suspect get away with behavior such as this. If your suspect starts to be aggressive or overly confrontational with their verbiage, they could be attempting to distract you and mask their true intentions, which could be to flee or assault you. Drive the narrative of the conversation. Let the individual know that you control the conversation and that there will be no negotiating when it comes to compliance.

The courts are comfortable with the fact that police officers can take reasonable preemptive action against an individual that they believe is about to assault them. If your suspect is getting to the level were you believe they could be physically combative and you can't regain control verbally move to physically control them before things get out of hand. Change the location of the individual to an area more advantageous to you, repositioning the individual to a seated position or simply placing them in handcuffs can reestablish physical control.

You Must Never Hesitate

Don't hesitate to take control of your scene or to act on the behavior you observe. One of the traits of slain officers, the authors of the FBI study referenced earlier, found was that these officers were hesitant to use force. The murdered officers not only were hesitant to use force, but they used less force than their peers would have used in similar circumstances.[6] Drive the narrative and take corrective action immediately. Similarly, be decisive. Being indecisive will cost you time and could lead to you being killed or injured. The more indecisive you are, the more time you will give your suspect to think about how they will react to you. Suspects will recognize and take advantage of indecision on your part. Indecision will lead to costly mistakes. In the police world, I'd rather be decisive and wrong than indecisive and right.

---

[6] Chuck Remsburg. Traits That Get Cops Killed. Accessed April 18, 2016. http://www.poam.net/train-and-educate/2008/train-educate/

Three's a Crowd

While only having to control one person during a stop is preferable, it will not always end up that way. Oftentimes, you will be forced to control several individuals throughout the stop. Some could have been there from the beginning and some may have interjected themselves into the stop at some point in time. Not taking control of two or more persons during a stop can exacerbate losing control. Typically, the presence of another person can empower the others, and your stop can spiral out of control. This can create a dangerous dynamic. In order to prevent this mob mentality, many of the same techniques we are talking about can be utilized to control stops of more than one person. If the subsequent individuals are involved in the stop (not free to go), treat them as you would any other individual that you stop. If the subsequent individuals are not related to the stop or are free to go, advise them that you would be happy to explain the circumstances or talk to them after your business is concluded. Then suggest a safe place that they can wait for the individual. Stress to the individual that their continued disruptions are only prolonging the stop, and it would be prudent for them to disengage. I'll still try and position the person I have stopped in a manner that still allows me to observe the other individuals that will be waiting. Under no circumstances should you allow an individual that you have stopped to interact or make contact with another person. If you start to see this behavior make it obvious to all parties that, that behavior will not be tolerated. Tell the person they are free to wait for the person elsewhere. Drive the narrative of the stop and take control, regardless of the number of people. Be firm, authoritative, and decisive. Let whomever is there know that you're in charge of the stop and compliance is necessary. Aside from the logistical and safety considerations of additional subjects, your techniques and demeanor should not change.

The Good Samaritan

I want to share a story with you that touches on some of the topics we have been discussing. My partner and I were on foot patrol in one of my favorite areas of town. In this area, PCP was becoming more and more common, so we were out and about looking for individuals that may be in possession of the drug. We stopped an individual for a minor offense and began talking with him. He stood at about five feet, eight inches, making him shorter than me; however, he was about three hundred pounds. When most people hear a person is three hundred pounds, they immediately think that person is obese; however, he was three hundred solid pounds of mostly muscle. He was bald with a beard and looked like a popular MMA fighter that started on the Internet circuits.

When we initially made contact with him, he was very aggressive. He tested us early by shouting and flailing his arms about in an attempt to make a scene. Being familiar with this behavior, we immediately sought to correct it. In a firm and semi-loud manner, we instructed him over to an advantageous position and started to talk to him. He calmed down somewhat but was still a little tense. As we continued to talk to him, we could smell the odor of PCP coming from his breath. Fearing a physical altercation with the individual, we decided it would be prudent to handcuff him. When we instructed him to turn around and place his hands behind his back, he hesitated briefly. Seeing this, we slightly closed the gap, adapted a more aggressive stance, and immediately repeated the instructions. This time, he turned around and we handcuffed him.

Later on, we were able to locate a vile of PCP on his person. Of course he tried to convince us that he had found it on the ground and picked it up in order to prevent any kids from getting a hold of it. While it sounded noble, he was clearly lying. Before we left for processing, I looked over his criminal record, and it was littered with violent crimes, including attempted murder and assaults against police officers. I rolled down the window in the back of the car and noticed that he was shaking like a leaf. I asked him why he was shaking and why this encounter didn't end like so many of his previous encounters did, with violence. He told me that from the moment we had stopped him, he knew right away that he could not gain control of the scene. He stated that the way in which we controlled him led him to believe that if he were to assault us, he would end up on the losing side. He saw no reason to assault us because he knew he would not get away. It was a stark and honest revelation. Here is a three hundred-pound man who has an easy one hundred pounds of body weight on me, standing in front of me shaking because he was scared. Keep in mind, we didn't actually use any force or threaten to use any force against his person. The individual made a determination based on a series of observations about our behaviors and actions that led him to conclude that compliance was more appropriate. A physical altercation was avoided because we controlled the scene and did it early.

The suspects will attempt to control the scene. Allowing them to control the scene will not only make it unsafe for you but will empower them to continue with their uncooperative behavior. Passerbys might also start to interject themselves into your scene if they believe that you are losing control. The more

they feel they're in control of the scene, the more uncooperative and daring their behavior will be. If you don't run the
scene, the suspect will! Take control of your scene early. You'll
be safer because of it.

CHAPTER

5

Legal

At this point, if you are reading this book, you should already be interested in or have some basic knowledge regarding the laws and procedures in the United States regarding police interactions. This book is not designed as a legal guide so we'll just briefly touch on some of these cases as more of a contextual basis.

Your success as a police officer will largely depend on your ability to properly navigate and utilize the law. It's important that you learn to work within the confines of the law and learn to apply the various legal principles properly so that your case will reach a successful resolution. Your acumen in performing stops will be useless if you can't perform them within the confines of the law.

Before we get into the nuts and bolts of how to stop a person, we first need to explore a few legal concepts regarding the stop, seizure, and subsequent searching of an individual. Since a stop is usually the first interaction we will have with our suspects, we want to make sure that the stop is done legally. This is important because if our stop is deemed to be illegal, any evidence contained thereafter can fall under the exclusionary rule and be inadmissible in court. What is the exclusionary rule? The exclusionary rule arose from the case of Mapp v. Ohio and basically states that any evidence obtained illegally can't be used in court.[7] Constructing the stop in a legal way will ensure the veracity of our case and ensure that the rights afforded to all Americans by the 4th amendment of the US Constitution are respected.

The concept of a stop arose from the case of Terry v. Ohio. In that case, the defendant (Terry) was casing a store while being kept under surveillance by detectives. Terry was stopped before he committed a crime. During the questioning, Terry appeared nervous and was making furtive gestures. The detective subsequently patted down the outer garments of Terry's clothing and felt what he believed to be a gun.

The detective reached into Terry's clothing and removed the aforementioned handgun. Terry was arrested and appealed his conviction based on the fact that the search of his person has unconstitutional because the police lacked probable cause to stop him and did not possess a warrant to search him. The courts held that the stop and pat down of Terry was constitutional.[8] They proceeded to establish a few boundaries that are important to us.

Reasonable Suspicion

Terry created the framework for what a "stop" is. A stop is based on reasonable suspicion. Reasonable suspicion can be described as "an objectively justifiable suspicion that is based on specific facts or circumstances and that justifies stopping and sometimes frisking (for a weapon) a person thought to be

---

[7] Findlaw. Mapp v. Ohio. Accessed March 29, 2016.
http://caselaw.findlaw.com/us-supreme-court/367/643.html
[8] Legal Information Institute. Terry v. Ohio. Accessed March 29, 2016.
https://www.law.cornell.edu/supremecourt/text/392/1

involved in criminal activity at the time of the stop".[9] The key to remember is reasonable. The courts will allow officers a lot of leeway so long as the officer acted in a reasonable manner. This is an important concept to understand. *Reasonable* is a subjective term that will hinge on your ability to articulate why the action you took was reasonable. This will become critically important when you get to court and have to explain your actions in front of the judge or jury. The better you become at articulating why your actions are reasonable, the more successful the outcome of your cases will be. Your goal will be to paint a clear picture of the events surrounding the actions you took and really show the judge or jury that the actions the suspect took were so beyond obvious that you almost had no other option than to intervene. That the suspect drew so much attention to himself or herself and their behavior was so far outside of the realm of what normal behavior is that any reasonable officer would have intervened at that point.

Some factors that are involved on establishing reasonable suspicion are the presence of the suspect at a particular time or place. While it is reasonable to expect that individuals will be lingering around a restaurant during business hours, it is not reasonable to expect that individuals should be lingering around a business three hours after that business has closed. These actions could lead to reasonable suspicion for a stop. Furtive gestures will also help you build reasonable suspicion especially during a stop. Observing furtive movements during a stop can certainly lead to the reasonable suspicion necessary to justify a Terry pat down. Reaction when seeing the police can lead to reasonable suspicion to conduct a stop. As we'll see in Minnesota v. Dickerson, the courts ruled that it was suspicious

[9] Findlaw. Reasonable Suspicion. Accessed May 2, 2016. http://dictionary.findlaw.com/definition/reasonable-suspicion.html

that when the suspect saw the police, he turned and started walking in the opposite direction. The courts ruled that, that was a factor in the formation of the reasonable suspicion involved to stop Dickerson.[10] Likewise, if a suspect sees the police and immediately flees, the courts have determined that, that behavior can lead to reasonable suspicion to stop the suspect for further investigation. Perhaps one of the most obvious forms of reasonable suspicion is if a suspect matches the description of a lookout. As long as you can articulate why the suspect matched the lookout of the person you are looking for, reasonable suspicion exists for a stop. Remember the phrase *reasonable*. The suspect doesn't have to match the lookout exactly; however, you better be prepared to explain your actions and observations if you stop an individual that varies from the lookout slightly. This typically isn't a problem because the courts understand that there are variances in the information that police officer receive from communications and citizens and suspect descriptions might vary slightly or have been altered.

Reasonable suspicion is a threshold that is less than probable cause but more than just a hunch. A stop, therefore, is not an arrest but an investigatory detention. A stop should be brief in nature (forty-five minutes or less) and the sole purpose of stop should be to determine if there is probable cause to believe that a crime has been committed. If you cannot determine that probable cause exists for further action, the subject is to be released. Keep in mind that unless you have probable cause established from one of the warrantless search exceptions, which we will cover later, you cannot search a person on the basis of reasonable suspicion alone

---

[10] Legal Information Institute. Minnesota v. Dickerson. Accessed March 28, 2016.
https://www.law.cornell.edu/supct/html/91-2019.ZO.html

We Only Pat Down for Weapons!

The most important item I want you to take away from Terry and remember while out on patrol is that a pat down conducted under Terry is for weapons only. I observed a lot of officers err in their understanding of Terry by stopping an individual and patting them down only to feel and retrieve some other item such as narcotics. This presents another issue entirely, and we will discuss it when we explore Minnesota v. Dickerson. For now, it is important to understand that a Terry stop and pat down is only valid if you believe the suspect has a weapon. When determining if you can conduct a Terry pat down, you must have some reasonable and articulable reasons that you would lead you to believe that the suspect is armed. These factors can be furtive gestures the suspect has been making, the nature of crimes that are committed in the area in which you have spotted the suspect, your experience level encountering armed individuals, the reputation of the subject you have stopped, discernible bulges in the suspect's clothing, witness statements, clothing inconsistent with the weather conditions, etc.

Remember, Terry is not a search; it is a pat down of the outer clothes. The only way you can go further than the outer layer is if you feel what you believe to be a weapon. (If the subject has multiple layers or a very bulky jacket, some courts have held that you can push those layers to the side for your pat down). In that case, you can retrieve from the person whatever you have determined to be a weapon. If in the course of retrieving that item you discover some other contraband, that contraband is considered to have been legally seized. Don't get yourself into trouble by abusing this rule. The courts put a lot of weight into an officer's experience level. Don't spit in the face of the court by ignoring these factors and stretching them beyond the means they are intended to be. I've have seen officers get into trouble when they remove contraband that clearly are not weapons. You must be able to articulate why you thought the item you removed was a weapon. The court will wrap this in the veil of reasonableness. It is reasonable to assume that an item that has a hard metal frame with a handle is a handgun. It is much more precarious to argue that a baggie containing heroin was a weapon and needed to be removed. Now if in the course of removing the handgun a baggie of heroin fell to the ground, the heroin would be legally seized.

Plain Feel

That brings me a one of the limitations on a Terry stop. The case Minnesota v. Dickerson involves the distinction between a pat down and a manipulation of items in a person's pocket. In Minnesota v. Dickerson, two patrol officers were patrolling an area known to have a high level of drug activity, particularly in crack cocaine. The officers observed an individual exit a known crack house and start walking in the direction of the police cruiser. When the individual saw the police cruiser, he turned around and started to walk in the opposite direction. Thinking this was suspicious, the officers exited the cruiser and stopped Dickerson. During the course of the stop, the officers determined that there were grounds for a Terry pat down. During the pat down, one of the officers testified that he felt a small lump in Dickerson's pocket. He went on to say that he manipulated the small object between his fingers multiple times and had determined based on his experience that the object more likely than not was crack cocaine.

He retrieved the object, and it was indeed crack cocaine. Dickerson was convicted, and the courts subsequently overturned his conviction. They held that although the factors establishing the Terry pat down were correct, the manipulation of the object by the officer constituted a search and was therefore unconstitutional. The courts determined that unless the officer immediately recognized that the item was contraband without manipulation, any further manipulation was unconstitutional.[11] The standard set by the court in whether or not the officer can immediately identify the object as contraband is indeed a very high threshold to meet. Some objects like pipes for smoking marijuana or crack cocaine are easily recognizable as contraband. On the other hand, some objects like baggies of narcotics are much harder to articulate as immediately recognizable as contraband.

This is an important case for us because it correctly limits the scope of a Terry pat down. Remember, when stopping and patting individuals down under Terry, the primary reason is to determine if they are armed. The pat down can lead to the seizure of other items, but there must not be any object manipulation.

Probable Cause

For an arrest to be made, there must be probable cause. Probable cause is defined as "articulable facts and circumstances that would lead a reasonable police officer, in the light of his or her training and experience, to believe that a particu-

---

[11] Legal Information Institute. Minnesota v. Dickerson. Accessed March 28, 2016.
https://www.law.cornell.edu/supct/html/91-2019.ZO.html

lar person has committed, is committing, or is about to commit a crime".[12] Probable cause is also needed in most circumstances to lead to one of the warrantless search exemptions required for searching a subject. Remember, probable cause is not definitive cause. The standard of probable cause rests on our favorite word, *reasonableness*. Make sure your actions are reasonable and can be articulated and defended in court.

An important legal concept in the formulation of probable cause we need to discuss is the concept of "totality of circumstances," which arose from the case of Gates v. Illinois. The case centered on the information that the police used in obtaining a search warrant for the defendant's home and vehicle. The courts threw out an older two-pronged test for determining of probable cause existed and created a new legal concept called the totality of circumstances. The courts stated that "the task of the issuing magistrate is simply to make a practical, common sense decision whether, given all the circumstances set forth in the affidavit before him, there is a fair probability that contraband or evidence of a crime will be found in a particular place".[13]

When I spoke about "painting a picture" of the events surrounding your stop, I was talking about the totality of circumstances. These will include direct factual perceptions like sight, sound, smell, hearing, information from witness, informants, other officers, reactions of K-9 dogs, any physical evidence that is available, and the officer's training and experience level. The court will take all these factors into consideration when determining if probable cause exists for an arrest.

---

[12] Findlaw. Probable Cause. Accessed May 2, 2016.
http://criminal.findlaw.com/criminal-rights/probable-cause.html
[13] Justia. Illinois v. Gates. Accessed March 29, 2016.
https://supreme.justia.com/cases/federal/us/462/213/

JEREMY GUIDA

The experience level of the officer is going to weigh heavily by the courts. As we will discuss in the courts section, you must become an expert in your case. The courts will expect you to be highly informed in your case, and it will be your duty to present the information to them in a clear and concise manner. They'll look to you as an expert on the subject matter.

Searches

As we are conducting stops, it is important to remember when we can and can't search an individual. A lot of your arrests will come from stops and subsequent searches of your individuals. Before we delve deeper into the art of stops, we need to explore our boundaries regarding when we can and can't search an individual.

The Fourth Amendment of the Bill of Rights states, "The right of the people to be secure in their persons, houses, papers, and effects, against unreasonable searches and seizures, shall not be violated, and no warrants shall issue, but upon probable cause, supported by oath or affirmation, and particularly describing the place to be searched, and the persons or things to be seized".[14] While it is crucial that we follow the Fourth Amendment over the years, the courts have made multiple exceptions to the warrant requirements of the Fourth Amendment. Since we will be focusing the majority of this book on patrol procedures, we will focus extensively on the warrantless search exemptions. While there may be a time where you will seek search warrants through a judge or magistrate when dealing in individual person stops, the majority of our searches will fall under the exemptions to the warrant requirement of the

---

[14] Legal Information Institute. Fourth Amendment. Accessed May 2, 2016. https://www.law.cornell.edu/constitution/fourth_amendment

Fourth Amendment. There are typically thirteen recognized warrantless search exemptions. They are as follows: exigent circumstances, Terry pat downs, search incident to arrest, plain view, custodial searches in processing facilities, border searches, vehicle searches, abandon property, open fields, probation/parole, consent, protective sweeps, and administrative searches.[15]

It's important that we understand the exemptions and learn how they can be applied during the course of our stops. In this section, we'll simply state the exemptions and then as we progress through the chapter on the art of the stop, we will reintroduce the various exemptions and highlight specific examples of the most frequently employed exemptions.

The first exemption to the warrant requirement is when emergency or exigent circumstances present themselves. This was put in place to allow officers to search when they don't have the time to obtain a search warrant due to emergency circumstances such as the following: there is a person in immediate need of police assistance and not providing that assistance to the individual would result in physical danger or harm, when evidence may be or is being destroyed and it would be inappropriate to obtain a search warrant because by then the evidence would've been destroyed or discarded, when there is the possibility of an escape risk, or when you are in hot pursuit of a felon. This requirement for the most part is the degree of urgency involved and how the time it would take to get a warrant would negatively impact the circumstances.

The second exemption has already been previously discussed and is a Terry pat down. As you've already known, a

---

Terry pat down doesn't require that you have a search warrant; it only requires reasonable suspicion to believe the subject is armed. Also keep in mind that a Terry pat down can extend to the immediate area within the individual's "wingspan." These areas can include backpacks or purses (you must still remember you can only pat down the outer areas of these items, not open them and search their contents) or the driver or passenger area of a vehicle you removed them from.

The third exemption is search incident to arrest. This type of search is fairly obvious. After a custodial arrest, you have the ability to search the person completely to ensure they have no other contraband and to ensure their property is properly catalogued. Really, the only threshold that needs to be met for a search incident to arrest is a valid custodial arrest. Some jurisdictions offer the suspect the ability to be released on a summons or citation at the scene of the stop, by the officer. A search incident to arrest would not typically apply in these circumstances because the issuance of a summons or citation is not considered a custodial arrest. Included in search incident to arrest is the wingspan of the arrestee to include the passenger area of a vehicle and in most circumstances any area reasonably within the suspect's wingspan where they could have stashed evidence.

The fourth exemption, and it is one we will go into detail about later, is the plain-view doctrine. This simply states that as along as an officer is in an area where he or she has the legal authority or right to be in, they can seize any illegal contraband that is in plain view of them. Keep in mind, tools we may use to enhance our senses must be readily available for use by the public. For example, binoculars are fine to use, but using thermal imaging to search an individual's house is not considered plain view.

The fifth exemption is a custodial search in an arrest processing facility. This closely mirrors the search incident to arrest. It allows for arrestees and inmates to be searched in jails and processing facilities without a warrant.

The sixth exemption is border searches. When crossing an international border to or from the United States, you do not have an expectation of privacy and can be searched without a warrant.

The seventh exemption revolves around vehicles and includes the Carroll Doctrine. This applies to any vehicle that can be used for transportation, including motor vehicles, boats, and motor homes. The courts have ruled because of the inherent ability of a vehicle to be driven away or moved from the scene; if an officer believed contraband to be located in the vehicle, the vehicle could be searched. It would be inappropriate to obtain a warrant because the vehicle could simply drive away. Keep in mind, you must have some other articulable reason that you believe evidence to be in the vehicle. Another exemption to the warrant requirement concerning vehicles is an inventory search. This, too, will be a useful tool for many patrol officers. If the driver of the vehicle has been arrested and the vehicle needs to be impounded for safekeeping, the officer can search the entire vehicle for the express purpose of inventorying its contents to ensure that any property in the vehicle is properly catalogued and returned to the driver or owner.

The eighth exemption is abandoned property. The court has ruled that individuals cannot exert control, property, or privacy rights to property that they have willfully abandon. This is another exemption that we will discuss in further detail later on. This exemption is especially important when we recover property that was discarded during a foot pursuit.

The ninth is the open fields exemption. This states that any open field not used for dwelling whether specifically marked or not can be searched without a warrant. This applies mostly to searches for narcotics.

The tenth is a probation or parole search. The release conditions of most inmates specifically state that they're subject to search of their person or residence at any time without a warrant. This type of search is usually reserved for the probation or parole officer exclusively. It typically does not apply to any police officer. Nevertheless, if you stop an individual that is on probation or parole and you can't determine any other grounds for a search, feel free to contact their probation officer and see if you can work something out with him or her.

The eleventh exemption is a consent search. This is a very important exemption that we will be covering extensively. In my opinion, this is the exemption that most patrol officers will deal with most frequently. The crucial thing to remember with this exemption is that in order for consent to be granted, the person must be free to leave. If a person is seized or stopped, they cannot give consent to search. Additionally, consent can be withdrawn at any time, but it must be explicitly withdrawn. The person can't be ambiguous with their language. Statements such as "are you done yet" or "this is taking too long" are not explicit.

The twelfth exemption is a protective sweep. This states that even if you don't have a search warrant for the area you are in, as long as you are legally in that area, you can conduct a quick protective "sweep" of the area, including other rooms, for safety reasons. For example, if you find yourself chasing a person into a house and you capture them in the living room, this allows you to quickly sweep the rest of the house for other occupants so as you're conducting your follow-up investigation in the house other individuals that may be in there can't pose a safety risk to you.

The last exemption is the administrative search. These searches take place in businesses that the government has a substantial interest in regulating and operating. As a condition of access into these areas, you can be searched without a warrant. These include places like airports and nuclear facilities.

This list of exemptions certainly is not all encompassing. I encourage each of you to do your own research on each and every exemption. Research the different exemptions to the search requirement, read the case law, learn, and exercise them competently. The nature of case law is that it is constantly changing. What is law one day may not be valid law the next day. The list provided here is only brief and only to provide context when we start discussing various techniques to apply while conducting a stop.

P A R T

Two

The Art of the Stop

Okay, we're just about to conduct our first stop; however, we need to further understand why we make stops in the first place. You will often hear other police officers, suspects, citizens, and media outlets diminish the work of police officers by stating that this or that reason for being stopped is "petty." As police officers, we get paid to be curious. If we have the legal authority to stop an individual, we should do the due diligence and stop that individual for further investigation. If it turns out that probable cause has not been established warranting any further action, we can simply release the person. The best way to deter crime is for the patrol officer to make sure they are doing their due diligence to the public at large and use the police powers that have been entrusted to them. Zero times in my career have I been approached by an individual that has simply handed me guns, drugs, or some other contraband. I doubt this will happen to you either.

You'll hear a lot of officers state that they are "waiting for the big stuff or this or that stop is to petty for me." This is the antithesis of what police work is all about. The basic building block of a case starts with the stop. Police stopping individuals for the smallest of infractions has solved some of the biggest cases. The son of Sam's killer was identified through a parking ticket. Timothy McVeigh was stopped for not displaying a rear license plate. The examples are endless but had the police officers in those cases not used the authority bestowed upon them, they never may have never caught some of those evil men.

You'll hear a lot about how to prevent or deter crime from police chiefs, supervisors, politicians, and whoever else wants to add their two cents in. The best way to prevent and deter crime is to be proactive. When criminals see active police out in the neighborhoods conducting person stops and being vigilant, they'll second guess whatever criminal behavior they had on their mind. When the criminals see police enforcing the law and stopping individuals, they'll be hesitant because they know that, that might be them if they are discovered. They might run into a confident, professional, smart police officer that will unravel their nefarious intentions and deliver them to justice.

Doing your job isn't petty; it's one of the best ways to serve and keep the public safe. If you don't stop people and instead depend on the radio for your calls you will not reach your full potential as a police officer. You will not learn the art of stopping individuals. A lot of officers make the misnomer of thinking that if they ignore the "small" stuff and wait for the "big" stuff, that when they get the "big" stuff, they'll all of a sudden be some kind of expert on arrest protocols. We've all heard that practice makes perfect. How proficient are you going to be at processing and working through an arrest if you never do it? If you only wait for the "big" stuff, are you going to be able to learn the nuisances of your local processing facility? How about the different procedures associated with different arrests, like drugs procedures, weapon procedures, domestic violence procedures? How are you going to fair when you go into court if you've had minimal experience testifying and dealing with attorneys, judges, juries, etc. Since you've had no experience because you only wait for the "big" stuff, will you botch your case? Will you have the requisite experience required to seamlessly navigate through the various parts of the justice system and make sure that justice is properly served? I ask this to every patrol officer: Next time you go into any processing facility, look at the recent arrest board and see what other officers have brought in. I promise you, you will see arrests for simple drug possession, disorderly, traffic, warrants, assaults, and a whole assortment of patrol related arrests. You will also see some robberies and more serious crimes but 90 percent of the arrests will be everyday patrol type arrests.

We're patrol officers; that's what we do. This isn't Hollywood where every day we patrol officers are solving the latest high-profile murder. Don't let that sound discouraging because we're always looking for the "big" stuff, but the difference is that the "big" stuff comes from the small stuff. Making the small stops and building the small stops into the big stops will gain you much more experience than waiting around for the radio to tell you a big call is coming or just stumbling into a big call. This is real life where the best deterrent to crime is active patrol officers.

This is a skill that can only be done through experience. Now you can learn different techniques, and I will do my best to help you learn through my mistakes and successes however at the end of the day you need to get out there and experience it for yourself.

Two for One

I want to share a story with you. This story centers on an arrest that my brother made. It will once again highlight the notion that regardless of the reason for the person stop, you need to take every stop seriously because only the suspect knows their true intentions. By the end of the story, you will see that the "big" arrests come from the small stops.

I was working with a plain-clothes robbery suppression team at the time. It was near dinnertime and the team had just gotten dinner. We walked out of the restaurant, got into our unmarked car, and turned the police radio on. Just as we were pulling out of the plaza, I heard the unmistakable voice of my brother come over the radio. He was out of breath, breathing heavy, and I could tell he was in distress. I immediately became worried because aside from the fact that he is my brother, hearing him on the radio in that manner is highly unusual. The only thing he got over the air was that he needed priority backup. I waited in anticipation to hear his voice again…

That particular day, he was on foot patrol in a nicer area of town. This part of town was known to attract individuals that were headed to one of the fancy malls in the area. While most people moving through just minded their own business, there were some individuals that would go to the mall to commit thefts and then move into the city and sell their "bounty." As my brother was standing around, he noticed an individual that hopped over the turnstile in the metro station. He approached and subsequently stopped the individual. He had another officer with him, but at the time, he was preoccupied on his phone. As my brother began to speak with the individual, he could tell right away that he was nervous. His eyes were wildly darting around, and he was rushing his answers. My brother observed that the individual had a sizable bulge in his pants pocket. He asked the individual if he had a weapon, and he retrieved from his pocket a large folding knife. My brother recovered the knife from the individual but noticed that the individual was still on edge. As the stop progressed further, the individual started to tremble and shake. He kept making additional furtive gestures toward his waistband, including what my brother believed to be a security pat. My brother suspected that the individual might be armed based on his behavioral indicators. He instructed the individual to turn around, and he proceeded to engage in a Terry pat down.

As the individual was turned around, he continued to take his hands off his head in an attempt to put them near his waistband. My brother reached around to the front of the individual, right above where his belt buckle would be and felt the grip of a handgun. Immediately, the individual tried to pull away. My brother grabbed him, dragged him to the ground, and the fight was on. It was a few seconds into the fight when the other officer, who was still on his phone, realized what was happening. My brother started to deliver body strikes to the individual. The individual continued to reach for the handgun, but my brother was preventing him from doing so. My brother was able to get him onto the ground and began to furiously deliver elbow strikes to the individuals face to disable him. While on the ground, the individual had his hand on the weapon and his finger on the trigger, attempting to remove the handgun from his waistline. The other officer was able to control his arm, preventing him from accessing the handgun. My brother was able to pepper spray the individual in the meantime.

My brother was finally able to gain control of the individual after OC was utilized and got him into handcuffs. The weapon was removed, and the individual was released to the custody of the other officer while my brother was being seen by the medics. As the individual was sitting there on the ground, my brother noticed that the individual was squirming and shifting around in an unusual manner. He told another officer from another department about his observations and the other officer immediately went over to the individual and searched him. It turns out that the other officer didn't recognize the squirming behavior of the individual as anything significant. The officer from the other department searched the individual and found an additional handgun that was secreted in the individual's groin area.

With one minor stop, two handguns were recovered. As it turns out, the individual also had a felony warrant for his arrest. What he was doing with two handguns that day we'll never know, but what we do know is this: you don't know the story of each person you are stopping. They could be a hardened criminal that just committed murder, or they could be a kid just messing around. You need to take every stop just as seriously. When you look at a lot of different police shootings, you will find that a lot of those incidents start over stops for minor offenses. I can't underscore the importance of making the small stops, and this is yet another example where a small stop bore fruit.

Just as important a lesson as building small stops into big stops is so too is another. Know whom you are working with and know that you can trust them. Know the capabilities of that officer and what they are and aren't capable of doing. Who knows how different the stop may have been if that other officer simply hung the phone up and walked over to the stop from the start. By the grace of God, my brother was lucky. One small slip of the finger and that stop could've gone much differently. My brother made it out that day with nothing other than a few bruises and a hell of a story.

Throughout the course of this section, we will discuss the various techniques for stopping individuals. Before we get into specifics, I want to highlight a few skills that we'll use in every stop no matter the offense. We will briefly touch on these skills here and then throughout the rest of the section we will explore these skills a little more in depth. Mastering these skills will allow you to build a solid foundation for stopping individuals.

Pay Attention!

As we begin or patrol career, we must relearn how to pay attention. Police work is much different than other careers. It's a career that requires our vigilance for every minute of our shift. As you progress in your career, you will pay attention to different things. You will develop a baseline of normal activity that occurs in your patrol area. Limit your distractions. Keep your head up and out of your phone. We've seen recently a large increase in ambush-style police shootings. Now more than ever, your head needs to be on a swivel and you need to always be monitoring your surroundings.

There is another form of paying attention that I want to talk about that revolves around stops. This skill will be invaluable when you start to stop people. As we get into the subsequent sections, you will learn what to start paying attention to. You will begin to use your attention and observations to develop reasonable suspicion, probable cause, plain view stops, etc. As you are physically stopping and approaching people, start paying attention to them. Pay attention to their movements, their demeanor, and their body language. Look to see if they have any signs of carrying a weapon, carrying drugs, or any sort of contraband. Start paying attention to what they are holding or if they have any bags. Start to pay attention to the immediate area around the stop. Did they toss something? Is there a stash of contraband close by? Know what you saw and be confident in it. If you have observed criminal behavior, don't let the suspect talk you out of what you've seen. Be confident in your observations. We'll get into more details later but for now, *pay attention!*

Don't Talk, Just Listen

This next skill we've been practicing our whole lives, but few people have mastered it. That is the skill of listening. Now I don't want to sound like your mother, but there is a difference between hearing and listening. Hearing is simply the physical actuality of hearing the words that are spoken to you. Listening is comprehending those words. As you start to make stops and investigate criminal activity, this will become a crucial skill. Listen to what people say. Start to listen for the inconsistencies and make mental notes throughout. When someone is talking or volunteering information, listen and wait until they have finished to begin your follow-up questioning. You will be surprised what people will offer up to you if you only listen for it.

Have you ever listened to a good salesman or a politician? What they do well is what we need to practice, and that is talking to people. They are masters at negotiating and driving the direction of conversations. To be successful at stopping people, we must master talking to people. Learning to talk to people starts with simply striking up a conversation.

Remember, you can approach anyone at any time and strike up a conversation. As long as you are legally where you're entitled to be, there's no requirement that prevents you from talking to anyone. You can get excellent practice by just striking up conversation with anybody. Practice approaching people and talking about things like the weather, sports, how their day is going, anything. This will help you develop a style and method of speaking. I approach my stops in almost the same manner, using as friendly a tone as possible. This may disarm the individual, and it will also disarm any passerbys that might be sympathetic to the person being stopped. I know its counterintuitive to a lot of things other police officers will say, but using manners and being polite, will open a lot more doors in terms of being able to garner information from individuals that don't want to give it up freely. I've talked a lot of drugs into my hands and garnered a lot of consent searches by just talking to people. Being able to effectively communicate with suspects will not only lead to more consent searches and more freely divulged investigative information, but it will also lead to less assaults on you. Being overly aggressive and confrontational from the start will lead to the scene becoming more tense, less safe, and will lead the public to turn against you. I've talked many people out of assaultive behaviors, and I've talked many arrestees into handcuffs. This has saved me from countless scenarios in which I would've had to use force. I don't want you to misunderstand me by thinking that I will not use force. I want you to understand that if you can affect the arrest safely without using force that is a much more desirable option. Learning to talk to people will greatly benefit your ability to effectively stop individuals.

Visualize Your Stop

Before you stop the individual, visualize the stop. If time permits, run the scenario through your head a few times. Scout possible escape routes if the individual flees. Scan the immediate area for anything that could be used as a weapon. Check for the most advantageous spot to make the stop. Start to craft the questions you might ask of the individual. As you are running the scenario through your head, start to conceptualize what your arrest narrative might sound like. Start to conceptualize what the defense attorney might ask about the circumstances of the stop. Doing this will enable you to mitigate a lot of legal challenges before they are even made. Your goal is to visualize and then craft the stop as seamlessly, safe, and as airtight for prosecution as possible.

Crafting Our Stop

Okay, so we're watching an individual and determining what kind of action we're going to take. Among the first things we need to decide is if we're going to conduct a consensual encounter or we're going to conduct a stop based on reasonable suspicion in which our suspect will not be free to go. This will be an important decision because depending on how we craft the stop this will affect the style and manner of questioning we use. Remember, the courts have typically ruled that it's the perception of the suspect that typically drives whether it is a consensual encounter or a stop. Now if we have a blatant violation of law or some other plain view doctrine item, our stop will go a little different, but right now, we are going to focus on the absence of some obvious violation of crime.

I prefer to craft each stop as a consensual encounter first. Keeping the stop as a consensual encounter will able to me use a full assortment of questions and tactics. Now just because I start the stop as a consensual encounter doesn't mean that I can't transition into reasonable suspicion. Likewise, just because I begin with reasonable suspicion doesn't mean that I can't initiate the stop as a consensual encounter. As previously mentioned, keeping the stop as a consensual encounter will afford me more options.

Since consent is in the mind of the person we have in front of us, we need to be cognizant of what we say and do. While the courts generally give police officers a lot of latitude, there are actions we can take that can invalidate consent and lead to the person being stopped and not free to go. Remember, in order to grant us a consent search, the person must feel as though they are free to go. If they're not free to go, meaning they're officially "stopped," they cannot grant consent. Keep some of these considerations in mind.

Watch Your Mouth

The language used during the encounter will be a key component in determining if your subject feels as if they are free to go. Remember, the person has to feel as though they're free to go in order to grant consent. You need to be sure that you don't use language that would indicate otherwise. Language like "stop" or "come over here." Actions like pointing or directing the person to a particular area could be considered a seizure. The courts could rule that behavior like that could be considered a stop. Instead, try to preface your statements with a question. Try "Can I speak to you for a minute?" or "Do you mind if I talk to you over here?" Using these statements, it's reasonable to assume that the suspect feels as though they can say no and walk away. Now in the absence of reasonable suspicion, remember they can say no and walk away. Don't take offense to this. Many persons will oblige and come and speak with you for fear that walking away makes them seem guilty but if no reasonable suspicion exists and they say no and walk away that is well within their rights. Don't let your ego get in the way and attempt to unlawfully detain them. It is not worth it. Respect their rights and live to die another day. There will be plenty of other people you can interact with.

What's Your Position?

In a consensual encounter, be careful of positioning the suspect. If you "handle" the suspect too much, the courts may constitute that you have detained the person and consent is no longer valid. I know we have a tendency to order people to stand here and move there, but remember, in a consensual encounter, they are free to do as they please. You can position them while keeping safety considerations in mind. Just like before, try and preface your statements with a question. Instead of saying, "Move here or move there," try "Would you mind moving over here so we're out of the way?" or "It's a little quieter over here, do you mind if we move over here so I can hear you?"

Again, keep in mind they are free to say no; however, most of the time, they will oblige and you can continue the encounter.

If you have additional officers with you, be mindful of their positioning as well. We have a natural tendency to "surround" the individual we are speaking with. This isn't nefarious; it's just a habit of our training. However the courts will take this into consideration. If we're conducting a consensual encounter and we have five officers surrounding the individual, the courts may say that the individual was not free to go thus invalidating any consent we're given. Be mindful of this sort of positioning. If you need to, try and have the other officers back off slightly in some overt way. We want the individual to feel as though they're free to go, and surrounding them could give off the impression that they're not free to go.

Time's a Ticking

A component to a consensual encounter that always seems to get lost in the details but can have significant relevance to whether or not your encounter is consensual or not is a question that has been drilled into our heads from day one of the police academy, "Do you have any ID?" This question is routine for police officers to ask but can have an impact on whether or not your stop will be considered consensual or not. In order to keep your encounter consensual, it is important to remember to relinquish the person's identifying documents back to them in a reasonable manner of time. Some courts will rule that if you possess the identification for an excessive amount of time that the person will feel as though they aren't free to go and consent will have been invalidated. It's still prudent to review the person's identification, but instead of holding onto it for the duration of the stop, try writing down their information quickly and returning the identification to them. I was involved in a motion to suppress hearing where the judge gave great weight to the amount of time that I was in possession of the individual's identification and how that directly related to the individual's feeling as if they were free to go or not.

Slick Willy

In the course of the encounter, if the individual asks you if they are free to go, do not get flustered. Get your politician hat on and simply answer the question but frame it in your terms, try something like "Of course you're free to go, but I would really appreciate if you could give me a few more minutes of your time." Use courtesy and manners to disarm them and to ensure them that you are simply there to talk to them in a friendly manner. That nothing else is on your mind, when of course you should be listening and observing for any signs of criminal behavior the entire time. Just keep in mind, if it's a consensual encounter and even after you say all of that, they still wish to leave they can in fact leave at any time without any further recourse.

Yes, Everyone Has Rights

The underlying purpose of most of our consensual encounters is going to be to try and get the individual to consent to a search of their person or property, like a vehicle or backpack. Before we get into some of the different tactics, I want to address an issue I see come up a lot. We keep repeating the phrase that the person must feel free to go and for good cause. Every person in the United States has a Fourth Amendment right against unreasonable searches and seizures. It is important that we respect those rights and go about our entire career upholding our integrity and the integrity of the US Constitution in which we all took an oath to protect. You can have an entire career of excellent, unblemished service, but it only takes one instance of impropriety to unravel your entire body of work. One of the most important things you need to remember when conducting a consensual encounter is, you cannot use coercion to obtain consent. By its very nature, coercion invalidates consent. The use of coercion could classify your stop as illegal. This could open you up to the possibility of administrative, civil, and/or criminal penalties. Not to mention you will tarnish your integrity and the integrity of every other police officer. It is simply not a gamble that is worth taking. Going about your stops in a legal way is much more satisfying than skirting the rules. Police officers are given a lot of leeway by the courts, and we have many different tools available for our use. Make sure you are conducting your stops properly.

Continuing on with coercion, I have heard officers say more times than I care to admit, "If I search you, will I find anything?" or more egregiously "I'm going to search you anyway so just come clean." These statements for the most part are considered coercion, especially the latter, and have no place during a consensual encounter. Remember in order to search any person, we either need a search warrant or need to have one of the warrantless exemptions. Without either of those, we cannot search the individual. If you use one of those statements or some other means of coercion, any evidence you obtain will fall under the exclusionary rule and will not be admitted into court. You don't want to go down that slippery slope. Nothing is worse than seeing a guilty person get off because the police didn't respect the constitutional rights of the individual and the evidence obtained was invalidated.

Not All Is Lost

If you find that upon your initial approach, you determined that your contact was going to be a consensual encounter, but due to circumstances, your contact has transformed into a stop where the individual is not free to go, don't sweat it. Your hopes of having the encounter be consensual once more are still alive. If you determine that you will not be arresting the individual and will instead release them, there is another way in which you can gain a consent search. After you have finished your stop and have given the individual their documents and items back, simply state to the person that the stop is over and they're free to go. Since they are free to go, they are once again able to give consent to search their person or property.

Before you walk away, simply ask them right then and there if you can conduct a consent search. It may be just enough to bail you out and allow you a search of the person after all.

Use Your Manners

When approaching the suspect, make sure you use a conversational tone. A nice friendly encounter will lessen the suspicion of the suspect that you are there for any other reason. Try and spend the first few questions developing a rapport. Talk about sports, the weather, local news, or any other easily relatable topic. All the while you should he observing the suspect for any contraband or any signs that foul play is afoot. As you are talking and developing a rapport, try and gain a little bit of information that could be relevant. Ask them where they work, if they live in the area, what brings them to wherever they are. Most importantly, listen to what they have to say. You can learn a lot about a person by just listening to what they voluntarily offer to you. We will get into that more in depth a little later. For now, we will focus on the goal of our consensual encounter, which is procuring a consent search.

Just Ask

There are many different ways to procure a consent search. After you have struck up a conversation and developed a rapport, you can try and simply ask the individual. Try the honest route and ask. You'd be surprised how many people will say yes. Say something like "We've had a large amount of weapons crimes in the area and we're just out here being vigilant, do you mind if I check you for weapons?"

They may say yes or they may say no. If they say yes, check them immediately. Remember they can withdraw consent at any time, so be mindful of that. In order for consent to be withdrawn, it has to be explicitly stated. It has to be a statement that carries with it no ambiguity like "You can't search me, or I don't want you searching that." If you hear something like that, the search is over. However, if they state something like "Is this really necessary?" or "Are you done yet? I have to go," this is more ambiguous and doesn't explicitly withdraw consent. Also, keep in mind that if you are searching them legally and you come across some other contraband that is not a weapon like narcotics, you are well within your rights to seize that evidence.

You can also use a little misdirection when attempting to obtain a consent search. If you suspect that the person has narcotics on their person but you don't have probable cause to search them, try a little misdirection with your questioning. If you preface your questioning in a manner that suggests you are looking for weapons, the individual might feel disarmed that you are not looking for drugs and grant a search of their person. I might even throw in my statement that we're not concerned about drugs in the area we're concerned about the recent rash of violence so you are out and about looking for weapons. This might be enough to disarm your individual. Keep in mind you actually are also looking for weapons and narcotics. If the individual consents to a search as long as you are legally conducting the search, any evidence you recover is admissible. Now if the person says no to the search, it is important to remember the mere statement of no doesn't indicate guilt on any level and cannot be used as some form of probable cause in turn allow you to search them. Simply put, no means no. Just move on if you have nothing else.

JEREMY GUIDA

Back and Forth

I want to share a case with you in which we ultimately lost, but it has some important factors regarding consent searches. The case started with my partner. He was aboard a train coming to meet me. The train operator had advised him of an individual that was passed out on one of the train cars and had not moved in several hours despite the train reaching the end of the line and turning around at least twice. My partner called me, advised me of the situation, and told me he would attempt to see if the individual would get off the train at the station I was at. My partner headed to the back of the train and attempted to wake the individual. The individual appeared to be disoriented whether from sleep or intoxicants, my partner was unsure.

When they pulled into the station, the individual and my partner exited the train. My partner ascertained his identification and started to run a warrant check on the individual. As far as I knew, this encounter was consensual, so I struck up a conversation with the individual. After a few minutes had passed, I asked the individual if I could search his backpack. He said yes and handed me the bag. As I was searching through the bag, I located a sock with almost two ounces of marijuana inside as well as a vile containing liquid PCP. We arrested the individual for possession of PCP and marijuana.

When the case went to General District Court the defense put forth a motion to suppress the search, stating that it was not a consensual encounter. I was the only one of us to testify during that suppression motion and the motion was denied. The defense appealed the motion to the Circuit Court.

When the case went to the Circuit Court, my partner testified. After his testimony, I remember he and the prosecutor exiting the courtroom shaking their heads. I asked them what happened and they stated they lost but intended to appeal the case to the Court of Appeals for Virginia. The case was heard by the Court of Appeals, and we ultimately ended up losing the case. The search was suppressed, and the case was dismissed.

As it turns out, the encounter was ruled not to be consensual but instead deemed to be a stop, therefore invalidating any consent search. The encounter was ruled a stop because of the manner in which my partner had the individual get off the train. Before the train pulled in as my partner woke the individual up, he ordered him to get off the train. Because of this order, the court ruled that a reasonable person would not have felt free to go. When they got off the train at my location, I assumed that is was a consensual encounter. The courts took the position that it doesn't matter if the officers feel as though the stop is consensual; it only matters what the individual feels. The entire case could have been changed if only my partner prefaced his order as a question and simply asked if he minded getting off the train. The most likely response from the individual would've been no, he wouldn't mind and the encounter from there would've been consensual.

Now I have shared this with you because oftentimes, cases can come down to simply one phrase or the other. The difference between winning and losing this case was simply a few extra words and a question mark. It is important to remember that when conducting consensual encounters, a reasonable person must feel as though they are free to go. If they do not, it is not consensual. If they say no, you can't search them. And most importantly, if they're free to go and just walk away, they're well within their rights. Live to die another day there will be many other individuals that you can interact with.

The Power of Observation

I want to talk about one of the easiest types of stops you will ever make. It involves the use of the plain-view doctrine. Remember from earlier, if we're in an area where we're legally entitled to be, any evidence we observe in plain view can be seized. It is one of the warrantless search exemptions. This type of stop sounds easy and generally is, but it requires the power of observation. As you're assigned to your particular patrol area, you will start to develop a baseline for what's normal behavior in your area. Where the power of observation comes in is when abnormal behavior begins to creep in. Studying your patrol area, the movements of the people, and the principal actors will help you to determine when behavior is not normal. Your goal is to develop your police instinct and pick up on these cues right away. Remember, we get paid to be curious. If you see something that looks a little off, observe for a little while and then make your approach. Nine times out of ten, when your instincts say something is off, there probably is. Don't make the mistake of rationalizing away abnormal behavior in your head. Statements like "While I know that looks weird, but it just looks that way because of this or that," or "Well, it's probably nothing, so I'll just move on" should never be in your vocabulary. When you recognize this behavior, believe what you've seen and go be curious. Some of my best arrests have been plain-view encounters.

Before we get into a few examples, I want to make the differentiation between a plain-view encounter before you have stopped a person and plain-view observations after you have stopped a person.

In plain-view encounters, before you have stopped a person, you have clearly observed an action that you know to be illegal. Before you even make contact with the individual, you know a crime has been committed, thus elevating the stakes of the stop. In plain-view encounters, after you have stopped a person, you may not have originally observed anything, but as the stop progressed, your observation skills have led you to some plain-view seizure. As we get into more examples, we will further explain the difference between the two.

It's Right There in Front of You!

The first example I want to offer is an example of a plain-view encounter before I stopped this individual. It was a Wednesday, midday, and an overall pleasant temperature. Not too cold, not too hot, a day perfect for walking a foot beat. As I was walking along, I noticed an individual with his back turned to me in a corner behind an elevator. The area he was in was removed from the sidewalk and was only about four feet wide. There was a half concrete wall to his left and the back of the elevator was to his right.

The area he was in was slightly remote, but more importantly, no person really had any functional reason that they would be in that area unless they were trying to conceal their behavior. He was about fifty yards from me, and I could see that he was manipulating something in his hands. As I approached him from behind, I turned my radio down a little lower and put my keys in my pocket just to be a little stealthier. As I got closer, I could see he was manipulating a spoon in one hand and a needle in the other. I immediately realized that he had just cooked heroin and was loading it into a syringe in order to inject himself with the drug. Now I was relatively new at the time, and I couldn't believe that in broad daylight on a busy street, someone would engage in this behavior, but as you'll learn, drugs have powerful effects on people, and they'll typically do whatever they have to do to get their high. As I got to within a few feet of the individual, I made my presence known to the offender so I wouldn't startle him and so I was still far enough away that I had some reaction time if he decided he wanted to attack me with a the syringe or some other weapon. I was able to seize the heroin without any trouble and discovered that he had additional baggies of heroin on his person.

There are a few lessons to be learned here. Some that are specific to narcotics we will cover later on, but the lesson for plain view is simple. Use your power of observation and be curious. It would have been easy for me to rationalize his behavior as something else and have never even approached him. I could have thought he was just urinating in the corner and have deemed it to "petty" for me to bother with. Instead, my instincts told me his behavior was abnormal; I was curious, and I made the approach. In situations like that, you never know where your curiosity will lead you. The "it's too petty for me" attitude would have lost me that arrest. While curiosity killed the cat, it will lead you to many successful arrests.

Three's a Crowd

In another example of plain view, I was riding in the back of one of the subway cars. I was in a separate booth that had heavily tinted glass, just observing individuals as they boarded and exited the train car. It was a Saturday night, and we were in a high drug area. I noticed a group of three younger guys get on the train. I immediately recognized that they were not residents of the area. You could tell by their dress, language, and overall demeanor that they did not belong. Thinking this to be curious, I focused on them a little more intently. They moved as a group to the back of the train car about five feet from the tinted glass that I was behind. They then got into a semicircle and started talking and giggling, which was strange because men don't usually giggle like high schoolers when together. I could see the tallest kid reach into his pocket and retrieve a medium-size baggie with what looked like bright-colored circular candies. I immediately recognized it to be ecstasy. The kids then started passing the bag around to each other and examining the contents. Just then, I exited the tinted glass and approached the group. I was able to walk right up to them without them even knowing, and sure enough still in plain view in one of the kid's hands was the bag of ecstasy. I subsequently seized the bag, stopped the kids, and elected to arrest the kid that was originally in possession of the bag.

Once again, use your powers of perception and observation. Start to develop that police instinct and listen to it when it tells you something is not quite right. When it does tell you that something is not right, pay a little more attention and wait for your opportunity to present itself.

It's about Time

One key to remember in plain-view encounters is timing. It's great that you have recognized abnormal stimuli, but timing your intervention to the stop is critical. It is ideal to observe your individual long enough that they'll eventually expose whatever illegal contraband they might have on their person. This next example will highlight the importance of timing your stop.

I was seated in my favorite viewing position, behind the tinted glass on one of the trains. I was in a particularly affluent part of town. It was a Saturday night, and we were passing through the bar district. It was about one in the morning, and all the drunks were starting to make their way out. I noticed a dopey-looking college-aged kid enter the train and sit right across from me. His seat was exposed, and I could see his entire body. As we began to move, he started to look around in a nervous manner. After he looked around a few times, he got up and took a new seat that was between two other seats where the view of his body was obstructed. He then reached into his pockets removed something and started manipulating it in his hands. I could see by the way his arms were moving he was "cutting" something. I waited few more seconds to ensure that he had fully exposed his narcotics and made my approach.

Upon seeing me the look on his face was priceless. I could see on his lap, he had a two-dollar bill, crushed up on the surface of the bill was a green pill, which later turned out to be generic Xanax, and he was holding a debit card that had the same green powder residue on the edges. I removed him from the train, seized the evidence, and subsequently arrested him. And oh yeah, it was his birthday and his lawyer mom was going to shred me in court (of course he would later plead guilty).

This particular case underscores the importance of timing. Had I jumped the gun and rushed out before he had gotten the narcotics out of his pocket, I would've startled him and walked away with nothing. Instead, I allowed him to get far enough long that he would have all the evidence I would need already exposed, giftwrapping the case with a nice bow on it.

Remember, when you are making these stops, timing is critical. If you have the time, use it. It's much easier and will benefit your case immensely when you can explain in your arrest narrative that you observed in plain view the defendant handling whatever contraband he or she was handling.

What's Yours Is Mine, if You Abandon It First

Closely paralleled with plain view is another of the warrantless search exemptions, abandoned property. This is a relatively straightforward principle that proclaims that we have no right to privacy to property that we willfully abandon. This can present itself in a variety of ways from property abandoned during a foot chase to contraband that is abandoned at the sight of seeing the police. The important thing to note is that if you have a circumstance where property is abandoned, make sure you can tie that property to the suspect. We will talk about this in depth in the foot pursuit chapter later, but in terms of person stops, be confident in your observations. If you observe an individual abandon property, after you stop them and retrieve it, don't let them talk you out of your observation. Trust what you've seen. When writing your narrative, make sure you clearly state you saw the suspect with possession over the property and then you observed them willfully discard it. Now you might be thinking that an individual would never willfully abandon or discard contraband right in front of the police, but as you progress further into your career, you will be surprised at the things people will say and do. Which brings me to my first example.

That's Not Mine!

I was on foot patrol in an area of the city that was known to be a high drug area. Heroin, marijuana, and PCP were all common. It was about ten o'clock at night on a Saturday. The weather was just warm enough that people started wearing shorts and T-shirts out and about. The area was dimly lit by a few street lamps, so it was easy to walk up on unsuspecting individuals and surprise them. The most common area for drug use in this area happened to be in the bus stands. Individuals would pretend they were waiting for a bus, all the while they would either use or prepare for use the drug of their choice. The interesting thing was that these individuals always choose the most secluded bus stand on the street to use their drugs. They were thinking they were being stealthy, but they were really just drawing attention to themselves.

This is one of the reasons we have talked a lot about paying attention to normal baseline behavior. Normal behavior is not to seclude yourself far from public view. However, normal behavior for individuals conducting narcotics activities is to seclude their behavior from public view. As my partner and I were walking the line of bus stands, we turned the corner and observed an individual, an older man probably in his fifties, in an oversized football jersey with khaki-colored shorts sitting in one of the bus stands. Aside from the obvious fact that he secluded himself in a manner in which was consistent with narcotics activity, he was also looking into his lap and manipulating an object with his hands. Now it was dark outside, so we could tell the object was not a phone or electronic device that emits light but something much smaller.

My partner and I repositioned ourselves so we were out of his line of sight and began to approach him. As we got closer to him, we could see that he was packing a marijuana joint. As we got about ten yards or so from him, he noticed us and tossed the contraband under the seat. We walked up to him, obtained his identification, and started to talk to him. Of course he had lied about the purpose for being there since not only did we observe him packing a joint, but also the bus he said he was waiting for was not running at that time at night. My partner then reached down and retrieved the evidence the individual had thrown.

When we presented it to him, he looked shocked that there was anything under the seat. The look on his face was almost as if someone else had placed it there. He tried to convince us it wasn't his, and it was already there. When we stated we had seen him throw it, he quickly attempted to convince us that he had thrown something else and that's what we saw. Knowing what we saw, we simply just let his claims fall on deaf ears. He ended up having some outstanding warrants for his arrest as well as being in possession of additional narcotics.

Remember, believe what you see. It would've been easy to let the suspect talk us out of what we saw, but we were confident in our observations and followed through. It highlights the importance of paying attention and observing your area for the baseline of normal and abnormal behavior. It would've been easy for us to ignore his behavior and simply walk away. Instead, we were curious and it led to an arrest.

Is Today Garbage Day?

Not every abandoned property encounter will be that easy. Some will require a little more work but nonetheless will lead to the same result.

I was once again in the same area of town. It was early rush hour around four o'clock. It was a very pleasant sunny day. I noticed an individual walk by me with a large black garbage bag slung over his shoulder. It stuck out to me because it is a little strange to be walking around with a garbage black slung over your shoulder, but nevertheless, not the strangest thing I've ever seen. I didn't stop the individual, and he walked up the street and out of sight. About ten minutes later, he passed me again, still swinging the bag over his shoulder. Now I was a little more interested because the direction he was coming from really had no landmarks or stores that someone would just walk up the street and return ten minutes later for. I still didn't say anything to him, and I continued to observe him.

After watching him for a few minutes, I observed him lean the garbage bag against a half concrete wall and walk away. Coincidentally, he walked right by me. At this point, I engaged him in conversation. I inquired as to his purpose in the area and asked him why it was so brief. He claimed he had been visiting the hospital up the road, but such a visit would've taken much more than ten minutes. After a minute or two of speaking with him, I asked him about the garbage bag. Much to my satisfaction, he claimed that he had never carried a garbage bag up the street. I pointed to the bag that he had abandoned, and he stated that that bag was not his. My partner stood by with the suspect as I walked over and retrieved the bag. I started sorting through it. There were clothes, boots, and a few other assorted personal items.

I then came across a blue makeup bag. It was about the size of a football and zipped up at the top. It was unusual for a man to have a bag like that. Frequently, heroin addicts will have bags like that to store all the associated paraphernalia that goes along with the addiction. I opened the bag and inside found multiple needles, melting caps, and multiple baggies, some containing heroin and others containing heroin residue. There were probably between fifteen and eighteen baggies in total. The bag also contained several pieces of paperwork that had my suspect's name on it. This helped immensely because originally he still maintained that the bag was not his. However, not only did I observe him with the bag, but I was able to tie the bag to him because of the presence of those identifying documents. He was subsequently arrested.

Once again, you cannot underscore the importance of making these observations and acting on them in a timely and appropriate manner. When dealing with abandoned property, trust what you've observed and make sure you tie the property to the suspect.

Let's Get to the Nuts and Bolts

We've covered a few topics that are relatively straightforward like abandoned property and consensual encounters. While it is still good police work what happens when the stop doesn't come as easy as that. How can we effectively stop individuals and build our case against them? We will begin to explore some of the nuts and bolts of stopping individuals, building a case against them, determining evasive behaviors, determining if they have contraband on their person, and how to respond accordingly.

Remember when we talked about the "little" stuff? Almost every single stop will start this way. Sweat the small stuff because it leads us to being able to establish reasonable suspicion for the stop and probable cause to take further action.

Play It Cool

When you first observe some criminal activity, let's assume for now it's a minor offense and not an offense that would require some immediate response, how should we approach the individual? Should we immediately rush to them and get in their face? I have found over the years that that method usually isn't too successful. By hyping yourself up and approaching the individual in that manner, the likelihood that they'll respond in kind is probably high, and you don't want to start your stop off with tensions that high. The individual might be more inclined to flee or be assaultive or verbally combative if you charge out of the gates in this manner.

I've found it much more effective instead to play it a little cooler. If I observe some criminal activity and I determine that I want to stop the individual, I might let them come to me. If they're already headed in my direction, then perfect. I'll just let them come to me. There's no sense in rushing them and spooking them if they're walking toward me. If they are walking away from me, I might try and find another route where I can get in front of them before they get too far away. If not, I might casually walk after them feigning disinterest so as not to spook them and close the gap as quickly impossible. When zeroing in on an individual to stop, try watching them with your peripheral vision. If you are burning a hole in their eyes with yours, chances are they'll realize that you intend to stop them and they may try and take some evasive actions. Watch them with your peripheral vision and slowly make your way in their direction. This will lead them to believe you may be interested in some other person and not them. This should allow you to get close enough to them to affect your stop.

Disarm Them with Words

When you make your initial contact with the individual, try and phrase a question to them. I might say something like, "Do you mind if I speak to you over here for a minute?" or something similar. This phrases your stop as a question and allows you to keep the possibility of a consent search open. Now of course if they say "no" and attempt to leave, and you have established reasonable suspicion and they are not free to go, then detain them. However, I have found that in most circumstances, the individual will oblige. When you are speaking, speak firmly but with a slightly lower volume. This will once again disarm the suspect. It will also make the suspect listen to you more intently. They'll be focused on hearing your words instead of focused on deceptive behavior.

When starting the conversation off, if you feel as though you need to disclose the reason for the stop, because they are becoming agitated, simply explain the reason. After I tell them the reason, I might then be slightly dismissive about either the crime or the punishment of the crime. I might say something like "Listen, you're not in really big trouble. It's just a minor offense that we have to check out. You'll be out of here in a minute." This will disarm the individual slightly, and I will usually remind them if they cooperate, they could be on their way in a minute and back to doing whatever they were doing in the first place.

Now the goal of disarming them is not to lie to them and trick them into thinking that you will not enforce whatever you stopped them for but rather make sure that the tone of the stop remains conducive to safety for all involved. This does not mean that you'll treat the stop with a diminished attitude or response for it's your goal for the individual you have stopped to believe these things. You can steer them in that direction. The point is to take the suspect's mind off the illegal activity he has committed and instead get him thinking about what he is going to do later or anything other than the stop at hand. Another simple technique for disarming individuals you have stopped is talking down the severity of the crime. I might stop them and say something like "You know you can be given a citation or even arrested for this, but I'm sure we can handle this without either of those happening." Once again, this allows the individual to think that he may be in fact on his way in a manner of minutes and will get them to be a little more cooperative to you.

Just Play Nice!

Make sure that during your initial approach, you remain as polite and courteous as possible. Remember that the goal of the encounter is to build a case. You'll get much more cooperation if you have a friendly demeanor than if you have a combative one. This will immediately turn off any possible channels for you to obtain a consent search or some other information that being cooperative would enable you to get. Just because you sound nice doesn't mean that you should turn off all of your other indicators. You still need to take officer safety into consideration but the point that I'm trying to make is that by disarming the individual you will create scenes that are safer for not only you but also the individuals you have stopped.

Another reason to sound as polite as you can is to do a little posturing. In today's society where individuals have been conditioned by the media and other outlets to associate every police encounter with the threat of violence or some other mistreatment, it is important to portray a positive image. Being overly polite will not only disarm the individual, but it will reassure any passerby that the encounter is indeed an encounter that they need not focus on because each party is being respectful of the other. It will give you emotional currency with your audience and will discourage outsiders from injecting themselves into your person stop because they believe you are committing some wrongdoing. This will go a long way toward your stop being interruption free and as safe as possible. As a bonus, anyone filming your stop will have a textbook example of a positive police interaction. We need to remember the big picture, and that is building your case beyond the initial reason for the stop.

Everyone Has a Job to Do

Make it clear to the person you are stopping that you are only doing your job. This tactic can work because you're in essence projecting your authority onto some other ambiguous force. It'll allow the suspect to think that your hand is being forced that's why you stopped him, not because of their actions. It'll also remind the suspect that you, too, work for a supervisor and are held accountable. You can reference that you answer to society, other citizens, or the legislative body of the jurisdiction. I don't make this or that law. I am only tasked with enforcing them. However, you can draw your ire to the city council. I might even tell them how to contact the city council. It is cathartic to them, and it disarms them by shifting the internal blame of the stop from you to someone else. It also gets them thinking in another direction and affords you extra time to visually scan them for signs of dangerous items, deceptive behavior, etc.

You Came to Me!

Make it clear to the individual that they drew their attention you. Oftentimes this is an effective tool, paint the picture to them that their behavior was so obvious, destructive, disorderly, blatant, etc., that you almost had no choice but to turn your attention to them. This also helps if you say others notified you of their behavior. If they feel as though or you convince them that their behavior was so egregious that you were forced to stop them, it might disarm them and let them self-reflect that they deserved to have been stopped. In their mind, it might shift the onus of the responsibility for the stop from you to them. They might even feel contrite. You can even push them slightly by saying something like, "Come on, you knew that would draw attention to yourself" or "You seem like a decent guy. Why were you drawing attention to yourself like that?"

Ask them to put themselves in your shoes. If it's possible try to relate to the suspect. Try to develop a rapport. Depending on your course of topic, it can also get their mind off of the stop and on to other topics. Regardless of the walk of life, every person can find a common ground to relate to. Try to talk about sports, their work, their family, other general interest items like relationships, schooling, hobbies, etc. Not only will this disarm them, get them thinking about something other than the stop, humanize you (making it less likely they assault you), but it can also be a tool for gaining valuable information about them. This information can be used in an investigative capacity later on. Gather information like who they live with, where they work, where they go to school, etc. Make sure as you are using this method, you yourself do not get engrossed in the conversation and still maintain officer and scene safety.

Each and every person responds to police a little differently. There may be a time were none of the tactics covered in this section work for you. That's okay. As a police officer, you have to employ a multifaceted approach. You have to adapt on the fly. If you need to raise your voice, then raise your voice until you get the desired result. Once they have settled down, return to your normal volume. Whatever the case may be, remember you want the stop to end safely for all the parties involved. While every tactic covered here will not work all of the time, the tactics covered here will work most of the time, so use them.

Disarm Your Subject, Not Yourself!

Even as you use a framework that is polite during your stop, be careful that you don't start becoming victim to the Stockholm syndrome. Maintain your vigilance and remember that even though you may sound compassionate or are even possibly compassionate, your entire goal is to disarm the suspect, not yourself. Make sure you still maintain control of the stop, including your subject's movements and be ready to snap out of that mode in at moment's notice if some other variable presents itself. You can be polite and firm but still maintain your command presence. Be firm with both your language and actions. This will demand respect from the suspect in a more covert way. I've found that suspects will respect a police officer that acts like a professional police officer, and this includes acting in a polite and courteous but firm manner. Don't make the mistake of thinking that I'm telling you to be "friends" with the person you have stopped. There is a difference between being friends and being respectful but firm. I have observed and heard of many stories where a police officer attempted to be "friends" with the person that they have stopped, only to have that person be disrespectful or combative in return. I'm not telling you to disarm yourself by being friendly. I am telling you to maintain a high degree of professionalism and to disarm the individual you have stopped to lessen the chance that they flee or assault you and increase the chances that they cooperate during the stop.

You Are Who We Thought You Were

Among the first things you should obtain when making your stop is the individual's identification. Aside from the obvious, which is identifying the person, getting their identification immediately offers additional benefits.

First and foremost, if the is individual identified they will be less likely to assault you. They'll also be less likely to flee from you. They know that they have been identified and fleeing or assaulting you really wouldn't serve much of a purpose because they will still have to face justice. It might not be that day, but rest assured, it will come. Getting their identification upfront can also help you in later investigations.

You Never Know When You'll Need It

A lookout was produced and disseminated to the members of our department via e-mail. The identity of the suspect was unknown at the time. The individual was wanted in a double stabbing and a mid-level quality photo was attached to the lookout. Shortly after roll call, I received a call from my partner, who was a hawk when it came to lookouts. He said he believed we had stopped the individual before and that I should take a close look at the photo. I opened the e-mail and took a look at the photo. The suspect was an individual that had a very distinct hairstyle. He had very dry hair with split ends, about shoulder length, and his hair was always an absolute mess.

As soon as I saw the hair, I immediately recognized the individual from an earlier stop in which I ticketed him for a minor offense. I immediately consulted my records and obtained a copy of the summons that I issued him. It was complete with a full name and address. Coincidently, as I called my partner to give him the information, the suspect walked right by him. He subsequently stopped the individual. Our criminal investigative division was notified, and by the end of that day, warrants were obtained for his arrest. The subsequent search of his bedroom located not only the bloody knife but also evidence of a cellphone theft ring. We used that information to recover over one hundred stolen cell phones and arrest multiple other persons.

Why do I bring this up now? To highlight the importance of obtaining quality identification on the persons you stop. You never know when you might need some information that you've gotten in the past. Had I not been thorough and obtained the correct information at the time of the minor stop, we very well might have never been able to solve the stabbing or the theft ring.

You Must Have Something I Can Use

Okay, you make your stop, and the first thing you ask is, "Do you have you identification on you?"

And of course, they respond with "no." Is it over? Not quite yet. Instead of phrasing your question in that manner, try asking them in a way that is not so easy for them to say no. Try simply stating, "Can I have your ID please?" or "Give me your ID." This is a little harder for the individual to say no to and signals to the individual that you indeed believe he has an ID on them.

We are conditioned to always look for that perfect scenario where every person we stop is in possession of some sort of government ID that is in perfect condition. People have many reasons to lie to the police about their identity. It's our goal to sift through the lies and accurately identify the individual that is before us. I worked with a guy that simply refuses to believe that any person is not in possession of an ID. You know what, he is right. Just because they are not in possession of a government-issued ID doesn't mean that they can't produce something. We just need to get creative. There are many different items people may carry that have their names on them. Other items that you can use to help establish a person's identity are other photo IDs like work badges, passports, school IDs, or rec cards. If you can't get the person to produce another photo ID, ask for something else with their name on it. I've used credit cards, library cards, SSN cards, EBT cards, mail, anything with a name printed on it. Now to caution you, just because they are in possession of any of these items doesn't automatically mean that it's their name on it; however, the odds are pretty good that it's them. It at least provides you with a starting point. If you're provided with one of these items and the person starts to make all kinds of excuses as to why the name on the card isn't them, then you need to start raising the red flag. People will lie to the police for many different reasons, ranging from stupidity to the possibility of open warrants for their arrest. Use your common sense and trust your instincts.

Lying to the End and Back

I had an individual one time go above and beyond the normal lying routine. I was on foot patrol in an area of town that was a high drug area. It was a Saturday night at around 1:30 AM, and I was just about to head home for the night. Just as I was walking back, an individual passed me. As he passed me, I was overwhelmed with the odor of marijuana, which was emanating from his person. This was at a time when marijuana was still illegal and smelling of the odor of marijuana was considered probable cause to search the individual. I stopped him and began talking to him. He immediately became agitated, which is usually a sign of some nefarious behavior by the suspect. I asked him if he had any drugs on his person, and he stated no.

As he stated no, he started arguing loudly that I stopped him for no reason.

I told him why I stopped him, and he put his hands in his pockets real quick and pulled his pockets inside out in order to show me he didn't have any drugs on his person. He must have forgotten because as he pulled his pockets out, out fell two pink zips of crack cocaine. I seized the evidence and placed him in handcuffs while waiting for a field test. The entire time I was waiting for the crime scene unit to provide the field test he tried to convince me that the cocaine was indeed laundry detergent, and he was on his way back from the Laundromat. Of course, when I asked him where his laundry was since he didn't have any baskets of clothes with him, he had no answer. Nevertheless, I asked him for his ID, and he said he didn't have one. I asked him for any other identifying information, and he said he didn't have anything. I asked him for his name and DOB, and he provided me with it. After the field test came back positive, I arrested him and searched him. During the search, I found an EBT card that was secreted inside of his sock. The name on it was different than the one he provided me. I questioned him about it, and he swore up and down it wasn't his card, it was his cousin's. He continued this lie all the way to the processing facility, and until his hands were on the live scan machine for finger-printing. Of course after the fingerprints came back, we discovered the name on the card belonged to him, and he had two open warrants for dealing cocaine.

The point is, that guy lied all the way to the end even in the face of overwhelming evidence. He presented every excuse in the book, and I very well could have mistaken his persever-ance with honesty. You will confront this type of behavior. Be steadfast in your determination. Trust your instincts and the evidence. Let the person you have stopped prove to you with evidence that what they're saying about their identity is true.

Let Me Get That Birthday First

A technique I have tried in the past that is usually successful is asking for the person's date of birth first. Most individuals, when they intend to lie, will come up with a name first and then a date of birth. Asking them the date of birth first may trip them up. If you ask them and they lead with the year of birth first, I would be a little weary. Most individuals believe that if they can convince you that they're under 18, you will not take further action against them. Convince them that this is not the case. Simply state that you'll take enforcement against them whether they're an adult or a juvenile; the only difference will be the processing. When they give you their DOB, do the math. If the DOB is different than what they are saying that their age is, then you have a problem. If you ask what their DOB is and they respond with an age, you need to be mindful of the possibility that they're lying. Asking people their date of birth should not be a hard question to answer. In fact, the answer should be immediate. If there is hesitation and it appears that they are formulating an answer, press them to answer the question as quickly as possible and listen for inconsistencies.

No ID, No Problem, We'll Figure It Out

If they absolutely can't provide anything with their name on it, we still have other resources available to verify their identity. If they claim they have had a license or ID card, you can run their information through the DMV database. If they come back with a valid ID, great; if not, present them with that information and continue on with your questioning. If the individual has a criminal record, there are usually databases available that allow you to pull up the relevant information. Some states have online public record databases where you can pull up anyone charged with criminal offenses. These can be great resources; however, they typically don't include pictures. Some areas have regional shared law enforcement databases. Information included in these might include arrest history, name, address, DOB, and mug shots. Using one of those options requires that the person have a criminal record. If they claim they don't have a record but you have a hunch, they do you can try to bluff and say something like "If you've never been arrested, what's this case from a couple months ago?" If they start to give some other answer, you can use that information and start to work backward. Be careful how you word asking the individual if they have ever been arrested. Being arrested could mean something different to everyone, so you may not get a clean answer. To some criminals, there is a difference between being arrested (processed in a facility), being locked up (incarcerated), being arrested but released on scene, and being overall stopped by the police. I found it best just to ask if they have ever been stopped by the police or if handcuffs have ever been on their hands and work backward from there.

I have in certain occasions contacted the person's parents to gain identifying information about individuals. This is especially important in the case of juveniles, but I've found out that it can work with adults as well as long as they are willing to provide the information.

If you have them stopped for a criminal violation or have at least reasonable suspicion, there are other methods you can use to obtain their correct information. Become familiar with the compulsory identification laws in your jurisdiction. Many laws state that of the police have you stopped for a valid reason you must present identification or else you could face arrest. If you have the person stopped for a criminal offense, remind the person that unless they provide you with an adequate ID, that they could face arrest. We talked about working on our speaking skills earlier, and this is a scenario where they would come into play. Try and convince the person that it is not your intent to arrest them; you would much rather either identify them because of procedural reasons (field contact paperwork) or issue them a citation and released them. The only impediment to your releasing them is a valid identification.

Spelling Bee

When obtaining identifying information from individuals, be cognizant of the fact that just because you spell a certain name a certain way doesn't mean they will. There are many different ways to spell common names, and there are many different names that you've never heard of. Make sure you get the correct spelling of every name. If you think they are being deceitful, make sure you press them. Inquire on the spelling of their names a few times through the stop to see if it remains consistent. Ask them for their middle name. This has tripped up its fair share of people. After I asked them, they just stared at me blankly and stated I don't know or I can't spell it. It's safe to assume that most people at least know what their middle name is and how to spell it. This will be important in determining if they have any warrants and if the stop proceeds further will make sure their name appears correct on all subsequent court documents.

So You Don't Have ID, What's That Then?

Remember when we talked about the power of observation? It should always be turned on. When stopping an individual and questioning them about their identity, pay attention for signs that they have ID on their person. If they're wearing tight clothes and you can see the outline of what looks like it could be an ID card, make sure you inquire about that. If they have a wallet on them, it'll be relatively difficult to hide. Most men keep their wallets in their pockets of their pants, so visually inspect those areas. If you notice the outline of a wallet but they state they don't have ID, present them with the evidence and adjust your line of questioning accordingly. If for some reason they have a wallet and are flipping through it to prove they don't have an ID, pay attention to the cards that are in there. Look for either an ID or some other card their name on it. The same goes if they are fishing through paperwork or a stack of business cards from their pocket. I've had many stops where they were fussing through some paperwork and a piece of mail fell out with their name or their ID fell out from the pile. Likewise, when you are dealing with women, look for signs of ID in their purse. Most women will walk around with their purses already opened. While questioning them, if the opportunity presents itself, glance inside to see if you can see a wallet or something you can use to ID them. Be observant, pay attention, and be cognizant of any signs of identification. Getting a good ID is the crux of good police work.

Liar, Liar, Pants on Fire

Now that you're a police officer, no one will ever lie to you again, right? They will be so enamored with the authority of the position that they will be compelled to offer you nothing, but the truth, right? Not so much. This will sound harsh, but it is the best thing you can hear; start with the premises that everyone is lying to you and let them prove that they're not. This isn't to say that everything everybody will say is a lie. However, now that you're a police officer, you need to make sure that whomever you're speaking to backs up his or her claims with evidence. People will lie to you, and they'll be good at it. We'll explore some body language indicators, different styles of questioning, and a lot of examples from my career to help you turn into a human lie detector.

People lie to the police for many different reasons. It's not our job to figure out why they are lying. It's our job to figure out that they are lying and take the appropriate action from there. Once we uncover a lie, then we can attack it and see what the underlying reason for the lie was. From the smallest stop to the biggest stops, I've had countless people lie to my face.

Non-Verbal Communication

Earlier, we discussed the need for you to learn how to talk to people. Now we will explore the need to watch people. Our non-verbal communicative cues account for most of the communication between two people. Next time you're out in an area with a lot of people, start to observe the non-verbal cues that others are exerting. Watch the couple in love staring into each other's eyes. Watch the arguing boyfriend and girlfriend. Watch the annoyed businessmen at the bar. Watch and learn those non-verbal cues. These non-verbal cues also count for police. It's important to note that just because the individual is displaying some of the body language indicators doesn't necessarily mean that they are lying. They could just be generally nervous about talking to the police. However, the presence of multiple indicators and other evidence should lead you to the conclusion that the probability that they are lying is high. Early on, in the stop, it's important to establish a baseline indication of the person's body language. Observe quickly what appears to be their normal behavior. Then as you continue the stop and question them, further recognize the abnormal behaviors that weren't present when you initially encountered them. This will help you direct your questioning based off the questions you observed the behavioral indicators after. Recognizing some of these cues can help you to determine if you're being lied to.

Why, What Nice Eyes You Have

One of my favorite targets to watch when talking to someone is their eyes. The eyes are difficult to control when lying and will betray their owner. A lot to do has made about the direction the eyes move when they are accessing certain parts of the brain. While this is interesting, I am not a psychologist. It is more important to us that we recognize these movements as a sign of deception and don't really concern ourselves as to why they're moving that way. When you're speaking with the individual, it is most common for both parties to make eye contact for a few seconds at a time then break momentarily and then reconnect. If you begin to speak to someone, and they are constantly staring at the floor, that could be an indicator of deception. If you're questioning them and they keep looking away every time you look into their eyes, that could be a sign of deception. If their eyes are darting around wildly, that could be telegraphing the person's intention to be combative or flee. If you are talking to the individual and they are just glaring at some unknown spot somewhere, that could be telegraphing their intent to flee or also could be signaling deception on their part.

An interesting subset of reading the eyes that can be very useful when you are talking to someone that may have illegal items on their person is what I call the visual security sweep. You've heard of the security pat when someone has a weapon? The same can be true for the eyes. Many times in my career, when I was questioning an individual, when I asked if they had any illegal contraband on their person, they would say no but quickly look away and directly to the spot on their body that they had the contraband.

If you are asking the individual questions and they are responding, pay attention to the head movements. Many liars will say no, but subconsciously, their body will nod their head and vice versa. It will look very obvious to you, and it'll help you direct your questioning.

I want to highlight an example that fits in perfectly with the "security sweep" using the eyes.

Are You Finished with That?

I was on working uniform patrol on a Saturday afternoon. We were in an area of town that was known to be a high drug area. My partner and I had opted to patrol using a vehicle that day instead of being on foot. It was mid-evening, right before dusk on a nice cool day. We were driving down one of the streets when we noticed an individual that was seated in a bus stand with the ominous white Styrofoam cup. Suspecting he was drinking alcohol in public, we pulled along the side of the bus shelter and got out of the car. I approached the individual and engaged him in conversation. This guy was a little slicker than the normal criminal, and he immediately recognized what

I was doing. My usual banter just wasn't working. Because the cup was unlabeled, I need to get him to admit it was liquor, or I needed him to hand it to me for inspection. Keeping in mind that even during a minor stop like that the Fourth Amendment still applies, and I can't just seize his property. To get someone to admit to me a minor behavior I just usually lead with something like "You know you're not supposed to be doing that, right?" in an almost casual tone. If they say something like "Yeah, I know but," it's generally considered an admission of guilt. But today, it just wasn't working with this guy. After a minute or two, the individual decided he was done with us and decided to walk away. He walked over to an overflowing garbage can and placed the cup right on top of the pile. Since he had abandoned his property and I was able to maintain an uninterrupted view of the property so I could tie it to him, I walked over to the garbage and retrieved his cup. Of course the cup was filled with liquor, and we subsequently made a stop of him. As I was questioning him, he was visibly nervous. I asked him for ID; he said he didn't have any. However, I was able to use his criminal record and look him up. As I was running his information, he got increasingly more uncooperative. Realizing that he was obviously nervous for some other reason, I started to ask him a few questions. I asked him if he had any drugs on his person, and he quickly stated no. Immediately following his response, he looked directly at his right pant pocket and held the gaze for a second or two. After he broke that gaze, I again asked him the same question, and he again stated no and glared at his right pocket for a longer period of time. I then noticed that there was a slight bulge in his pocket that looked like it could be a bag of narcotics. As a few more minutes passed, he became so agitated and belligerent that the only option left was to arrest him. After I placed him in handcuffs, I searched the right pant pocket that he was glaring at and discovered he had a little more than a half an ounce of marijuana in his pocket.

If you recognize this behavior when you are talking to someone, analyze your options for how to best retrieve the contraband.

The Body Speaks so Listen

If as you are talking to the person they're holding a steady, almost unbreakable gaze into your eyes and it doesn't appear that they are looking through you or zoning out, this too could be a sign of deception. A lot of good liars are familiar with body language and will try to throw you off. They'll know that they can make evasive actions with their eyes, so instead of looking away, they'll stare intently into your eyes. This behavior is them trying to overcompensate their eye contact. Next time you talk to somebody, see if they stare into your eyes for the whole conversation. I doubt they will. If you recognize this during your stop, be weary.

The body, too, will give away cues for you to help determine if the individual is lying. When questioning someone, look at his or her arms. If they're folding their arms across their chest, it could signal they're being deceptive. If as you are talking to them they start to perspire, especially if it is inappropriate, they could be lying to you. A key indicator of lying that is easy to detect happens when people touch their face. If as you are talking to an individual they keep touching their mouth, neck, cheek, or hair, they're probably being deceptive. This behavior will also present itself in the form of itching or scratching. It could also present when the person reaches up and touches the corner of their mouth. This behavior is usually the body subconsciously telling the brain that whatever left the mouth shouldn't have been said.

Why So Fidgety?

As we continue to explore body language, let's move to the ever so famous furtive gestures. You will hear this phrase used a lot, but what is it really? It's a set of body language indicators that can indicate that a person is armed. Think about when you carry concealed off duty? How many times when you first started carrying a gun did you touch it with your hand or hit it with your elbow just to be sure that it was there? You probably did it a lot at first just because it was a new sensation, but the behavior probably toned down the more you got comfortable. You probably walk differently when carrying, wear different clothes, and make different movements. Well, criminals do the same things and being observant to these behaviors will help you ascertain whether or not a person is armed.

When we have someone stopped, it is important to visually scan their waistband first and foremost for obvious signs of bulges. Also, make sure to scan any coat pockets and under the person's armpit in case they are wearing a shoulder holster. Now as you are speaking with them, you can notice subtle body language indicators that indicate whether or not they are armed.

Watch and see if they start to lean a certain side of their body away from you. Most people talk to each other with their shoulders square to each other. A person that is armed may slightly cant that side away from you. This is similar to how police stand when interviewing a person, with a bladed stance. The difference is we blade to keep our weapon side less exposed. The armed individuals will blade to try and keep any obvious indicators of a weapon concealed.

We always hear a lot about the hands and for good measure. This is where the security pat downs will come into play.

Jeremy Guida

If you are speaking with an individual and they keep either placing their hands in their pockets or touching one side of their waistline or keep one arm pressed tightly to their body, these could be indicators that the person is armed. If you observe any of these traits you can and should conduct a Terry pat down immediately or as soon as it is safe to do so. While most of these behaviors can be subtle, most will be apparent enough that your instincts should kick in and tell you something is not right.

Wednesday Night Special?

I want to share a story that illustrates a lot of the body language indicators we've been talking about. I was on solo foot patrol in a rather affluent part of town. This part of town had a very large upscale mall, which attracted both shoppers and thieves. It was my first day back to work after my days off, and I really wasn't in the mood to be working. To make matters worse, our chief had us in our dress uniforms, which are very uncomfortable and rather snug-fitting, especially for men. To top it all off, my pepper spray had leaked all over my belt and contaminated most of my body. I was walking around observing people when I noticed an individual that was just loitering in the tunnel between the metro and the mall.

This struck me as odd because the only reason you would be in the area would be to visit the mall and this kid was just kind of hanging around. As I watched him for a few minutes, he just continued to walk back and forth in a straight line, appearing not to be in a hurry to go anywhere. After a few minutes of this, I walked up to him and made contact. I asked him to step to the side and into an elevator, well, so we would be out of the main foot traffic. As soon as I walked up to him, he had the odor of marijuana emanating from his person. I pulled him to the side and started to investigate a little more. As I started to talk to him, he appeared very nervous. He kept shifting his eyes away from me and kept turning his hips from side to side. He would barely look me in the eyes and was almost whispering. To make matters worse, he kept touching the left side of his body right around his coat pocket area. As I noticed all these indicators start to spring up, I suspected he might be armed. I had him turn around and place his hands on top of his head, interlocking his fingers. As I was getting ready to frisk him, he kept taking his left hand off his head and kept attempting to bring it down to his left pocket area. I forcibly grabbed his hand with mine. As soon as I did that, instead of looking at me, he was staring at his left pocket as if in a trance. Just then, some of the plain-clothes officers assigned to the theft unit at the mall spotted me and offered their assistance. The suspect had a bubble vest on, unzipped, and a tight gray hoodie underneath. I moved the bubble jacket to the side, and I could see the outline of a handgun in the suspect's left hoodie pocket. I retrieved the weapon, and he was subsequently arrested.

As we've been stating, one of these behaviors is not that unusual, but once you start seeing several indicators appear at once you can rest assured that the person is being deceptive.

Listen to Me

We've talked about the need to learn how to talk to people and how to watch people; now let's talk about how to listen to people. Many new officers don't quite have this skill down. They will either go on these long diatribes themselves or as soon as the individual they have stopped starts to talk they'll cut them off. This is counterproductive. You want to keep the person you have stopped talking for good cause. The more they talk, the more likely it is that they will give up some information that will be useful to you. So listen to what's being said. During the course of the conversation, if you notice inconsistences, make a mental note. When they finish, return to the inconsistences and ask direct questions that require a response. When asking questions, try to stay away from simple yes-or-no questions. These are too easy to lie about. Also try and stay away from asking questions that answer themselves. For example, don't phrase your question like "That isn't yours, right?" You will make it too easy for the individual to lie to you. All they need to do is simply say "no." You're leaving them an easy out and making the chances that they offer you some freely divulged information slim.

Ask follow-up questions in a rapid manner. Most people trying to lie will only have a few rehearsed lines ready to use. To mitigate this, ask rapid follow up questions. This will keep them on their feet and make them answer quickly. This can lead to them making mistakes. Most people don't need a lot of time to answer simple questions; any hesitations in responses can mean deceit is afoot.

If as you are questioning the individual, you notice that they're hesitating too long before answering, approximately two to three seconds, press them for an answer. Don't give them time to try and craft a lie. Seize the gap and press them for an answer immediately. The same goes for if they start stumbling over their words. This is an indicator that you basically have them on the ropes. If they start stumbling, keep pressing the same topic or question, and it should lead to you getting a truthful answer. If as you are questioning the individual and they start to get a little quieter or start looking down at the ground in a somewhat shy manner, this could indicate that they may be about to tell you the truth. If they are speaking as they're displaying those signs, continue to let them speak without interruption. If they hesitate or pause, kindly encourage them to continue. Use language like "It's okay, you can tell me" or "It'll feel better once you get this weight off your back." Use language that is sympathetic and allows the person to feel as though you have some genuine concern and will help them through the process. If the individual is about to offer information that is useful to you, you want the information to keep flowing and them to feel as comfortable as possible.

Always keep them unbalanced during questioning; sometimes I will even alternate the content of the questions to keep them thinking rapidly. The more rapid the questioning and the more fluctuation and transitioning between the information, the more likely the individual will make a mistake.

For certain offenses, you can get the individual to admit guilt almost immediately. Try prefacing your question along the lines of "You know you should've have done . . ." (whatever it was). You might get a response that indicates guilt such as "Ah, man, I was trying to be discrete" or some other variation.

Be aware of qualifying statements. These are statements that add adjectives before whatever statement that they're about to say. It'll sound something like "To be honest with you, Officer" or "To be upfront about it, Officer." The use of statements like this could indicate deception. When you hear these, simply press the person for details. Call them out and simply state, "Were you not going to be honest with me in the first place?" and then offer them a chance to repeat their statement. Let them know that you have essentially caught them in a lie, but you are willing to let them start from scratch. If I hear something that I suspect is a lie, I'll have the person keep repeating it to basically let them know that it doesn't add up. You can even try repeating it to them and put a question mark on the end of the statement while giving them a quizzical look. This is a subtle way of letting them know you simply aren't buying what they're selling.

The manner in which they are speaking should be noted. Are they stumbling over their words? Are they talking very fast as if trying to rush you? When an individual is trying to rush you through the stop, this could be a sign of deceit. We call this manner of speech the warrant talk. People will talk so fast that you can barely keep up because they are nervous.

The Great Debate

A simple sign of deception that will occur to you quite often is when the individual wants to debate the crime. If you hear this behavior, they almost always are guilty. You might even get statements of guilt out of them right away. When you approach someone, they might say something like "I wasn't doing [whatever], or I didn't run that stop sign." This is golden because it basically admits guilt immediately upon contact without requiring any work from you. If they continue to press this topic, simply tell them that this forum is not the appropriate forum to determine guilt and that only a judge or jury can determine guilt. Or it is well within their rights to contest their guilt. A similar variation of this can occur when the individual will offer to pay for the crime upfront. In the case of shoplifting, they may contest guilt upfront but then say something like "Well, how much was it? I'll just pay for it so this can be over." This should be of interest to you because no one pays for a crime they didn't commit.

Say What?

Is what they are saying making any sense? This is perhaps one of the most obvious signs of deception. If you've observed the individual and have started questioning them and their statements just don't add up, press them for specific details and see if what they're saying makes sense. If it doesn't make sense, start to ask more follow-up questions, present them with the evidence, and start to unravel their lies.

I was on patrol late on a Friday night. It was an area of town that was known for literally every known criminal offense you could name. Drugs, guns, and robberies—it had it all. It was around midnight, and we had walked into one of the metro stations. The trains at this time of night ran few and far in between. The train pulled to the platform and one individual got off. He walked over to the fare gate and squeezed his body through without paying. The only persons in the station at the time were my partner, the suspect, and me. As soon as he had seen us, he tried to go back through the gates and pretend like he had paid. Ignoring this behavior, we simply motioned him over to us. As he approached, we could see that his right arm had been cut off right below the elbow. As we started to speak to him, he continuously tried to rush us through the stop. He was talking so fast we could barely keep up. He kept telling us that he had to get on his bus, which he said was waiting outside. As we continued to press for specifics, he became even more nervous.

What was even more telling is that no buses were running at that time of night anyway. As we continued to speak with him, he started to perspire. It was the middle of the night in February so it was not warm enough to be perspiring. We noticed that he dipped his right shoulder a lot lower than the

JEREMY GUIDA

left one. We thought this was weird but chalked it up to his having one arm. We also could smell marijuana on his person. As he kept shifting from side to side, we could tell that he was abnormally pinning his right arm against his body. With all of these factors adding up, we conducted a pat down. We removed a semi-automatic handgun and two additional magazines from a shoulder holster under his right arm. Using the current charges we had against him, we were able to flip him into an informant for our CID, and we used him on multiple gun and drug buy busts.

I can't stress enough the importance of listening. If we hadn't listened and just brushed that individual off, we would've missed out on all the arrests we obtained from using him as an informant.

The art of the stop is one that takes a lot of time and practice to master. There are no shortcuts. You need to get out and experience it for yourself. Start talking to people. Start paying attention to them, to what they say, to what they do. Start to establish a baseline for normal behavior and start to develop your instinct. After a while, you'll be a human lie detector. You'll turn small stops into big ones. You'll start to see the quality of your arrests increase exponentially. And you'll be on your way to being a formidable opponent to any criminal out there that is unfortunate enough to cross your path.

CHAPTER

7

Special Considerations for Drug Stops

There are many considerations that can arise that are specific to stops and arrests involving narcotics. We'll discuss considerations such as precautions when searching, physical characteristics of drug use, plain smell, decoy bags, and a few techniques when dealing with drug stops. It's important for you to become familiar with the different drugs that are prevalent in your region. This is not intended to be an all-encompassing look at drugs. It will be more of a general overview of some of the lessons that I've learned along the way.

Searching Considerations

The principal concern when searching anyone should be safety. This is especially important when searching individuals that you believe to be in possession of narcotics. Depending on the drug, there could be biohazard and cross contamination risks as well as safety risks associated with the drug paraphernalia that the individual is in possession of.

Before you start searching an individual, ask what they are in possession of. If they answer honestly, it'll help you get a better picture of what you're searching for. In addition to asking the individuals what drugs they are in possession of, make sure you also ask them if they are in possession of any other illegal items or any other items that could be dangerous to you like knives, razors, glass pipes, etc. I've stopped many wise guys that after I have asked them if they had a certain type of drug on them I've found some other drug. When I asked them why they didn't disclose the existence of the drug, they simply smirked and said I didn't specifically ask about that type of drug. Many criminals have subjective understandings of different drugs or illegal items. Make sure you're precise when asking what an individual has on their person. This also includes items that are not drugs but can still pose a safety threat. As you gain more experience, you'll start to learn what drugs you actually are searching for based on some of the characteristics that we will talk about.

As we discussed in the section on person stops, make sure you search the immediate area around the arrestee for narcotics or other contraband. Many times, individuals may ditch or stash narcotics or weapons very close to where they're located. We can't see everything all the times so it's important to give the surrounding area a one over. If you locate any contraband make sure you can tie it to the individual that you have stopped.

Check Please

When searching an individual that you believe to be in possession of narcotics, it is important that you are as thorough as possible. Drugs can be hidden anywhere on the human body and anywhere in a person's property. Don't let anyone rush your search. The last thing you need is to miss drugs and have them enter the processing facility or have the suspect attempt to destroy them in some other manner. I have found drugs in men's wallet between credit card slots, in cellphone cases, and in the battery compartment of phones just to give a few examples. I once discovered a small hole in the inside pocket of an individual I arrested with heroin. I thought it was a little odd, and since he was a heroin addict, I thought it deserved more attention. As I further searched the inside lining of his coat, I discovered that he had been secreting bags of heroin inside. After I exposed the interior of his coat, I had discovered that he stashed an additional fifteen bags of heroin in the lining of his coat. Drugs are small and can be easily hidden. If you're searching an individual and you come across papers that are folded up, make sure you unfold them carefully to inspect whether or not any drugs could be hidden in there. I have seen officers, many times almost discard of papers like that only to discover that they contained drugs.

If you have searched the individual and you have discovered that they had drugs secreted in some part of their body or you suspect that this might be the case, be sure and let the correctional officers or deputies at intake know that your arrestee needs to be searched more thoroughly. This has always been a courtesy I will extend to the processing staff. The processing staff have the ability to search your individual in private and more thoroughly than you would be able to do on the street. They cannot only find additional narcotics that you can include in your charges, but they can also minimize illegal narcotics from entering their processing facility. It's a win-win proposition.

I shared with you earlier the story of the individual that I arrested that was carrying and subsequently abandoned a garbage bag, which contained a pouch with heroin. As I mentioned he had a garbage bag that was filled with several clothing items and an extra pair of shoes. When we got to the processing facility, he kept asking me if I would allow him to change the shoes he had on and replace them with the shoes in his bag. Now I thought this was odd because the shoes he had on were perfectly fine. They weren't soiled or damaged in any-way. He must've asked me two or three times and the red flags started coming up. I started to realize he really had an interest in these shoes, so naturally, I wanted to know why. As I started inspecting the shoes, I came across a little flap of cloth in the side that had been cut and then folded over to create a little pouch. Inside of the little pouch was a folded-up paper towel that contained some prescription drugs, which the suspect had no prescription for. He was so adamant about getting those shoes because he had sequestered drugs in them. Remember, when we talked about being curious and identifying abnormal behavior? This was a perfect example. I didn't search his prop-erty as thorough as I should have; however, using my observa-tions and being a little curious about the motivation of the individual led me to recover additional drugs.

Just Stay Still

I know it's not fun, but when I say search everywhere, I mean everywhere on their body. I want to share a story that will highlight that point and another point we've been discussing. We've talked a lot about baseline behavior in terms of what is normal and abnormal. After someone has been arrested, the scene has calmed down, and they have been searched it's normal for them to sit still whether in the cruiser or waiting for a trans-port car. If you happen to notice after you've handcuffed and searched them that as they're standing there or seated in the cruiser they're squirming around or fidgety you need to con-sider the possibility that you may have missed an item during a search. Oftentimes, if you have missed evidence during a search, the suspect will be the most compliant individual you will have ever arrested. They may be talkative in an attempt to disarm you. They may be very quiet and mind their own business. The entire time they will be trying to make small subtle movements in an attempt to retrieve and discard whatever contraband they still have on their person. Immediately stop and search the individual again. I've been on a few scenes where after the individual has been arrested and searched they've attempted to destroy or discard contraband that was missed during a search. This can have serious consequences if the items you missed were a weapon. So if you observe this behavior stop and research them immediately.

Is It Really in There?

Now onto the story that will illustrate a few of the points that we have been making. I was training a new officer and I was in what we call "shadow" week. This is where I essentially shadow a new officer while they are on patrol. The difference is I'm in plain clothes and observe the new officer without providing assistance, within reason of course. As I was walking out of the bathroom, I noticed that the new officer had an individual stopped. I approached them and started listening in. She was attempting to ascertain this person's identity, and he had no identification on his person. She started to use many of the techniques we have discussed in this book to determine his identity. She asked him his name and date of birth. She asked him multiple times for the information at various times during the stop and each time he hesitated. When she pressed him to answer quickly, he gave a name and spelling that wasn't consistent with his previous answers. Not satisfied with his answer, she decided the best course of action would be to arrest him. She placed him into handcuffs without any issues, and I started to attempt to figure out who this guy was. As I was making a few phone calls, I noticed that the arrestee seemed really interested in the back of his waistband and kept trying to slowly creep his hands into his pants. He was in the process of being searched by my new officer, and she had the assistance of three other officers at the time. One of the officers was standing right next to the arrestee staring at him make these motions but wasn't intervening. I quickly made my way over, verbalized what was going on, and brought his hands out of his pants. I then searched the rear of the interior of his pants to discover that he had a bag containing eighteen baggies of synthetic drugs secreted into his rear end along with his identification. We later determined he had a pair of warrants for his arrest, thus the hesitation to provide us with his information. If your instinct starts to tell you something is off and you observe abnormal behavior, take action immediately. This can happen to you. Be cognizant and make sure your searches are thorough.

Learning the Paraphernalia Associated with Drugs

As I said earlier, know the drugs that are prevalent in your area. This will give you a heads up when you are conducting narcotics interdictions. You need to start to learn what paraphernalia are associated with each drug and what safety considerations need to be put in place. For example, if you know you will be looking for individuals that are in possession of crack cocaine, you know that you will have to be cognizant for glass pipes. It seems as though every crack cocaine addict I've ever come across and have recovered evidence from always has a broken glass crack pipe. Searching for items like that can be dangerous because of the obvious risk it poses to cutting your hand. The same can be said when you're searching persons that have smoked marijuana. A fair share of those individuals will carry around glass pipes and grinders. Considerations need to be made when dealing with either of those items. They can easily break and present a hazard to you. Similarly when you're dealing with persons you believe to be in possession of heroin, you need to be cognizant of needles. Most heroin addicts I've come across have had their needles capped or in some other container, but I have run into more than a few that have had uncapped needles just sitting in their pocket. Had I not taken the extra precautions and closely examined the pocket first, I could've plunged my hand into it and have been possibly contaminated. Cross-contamination with needles is perhaps one of my greatest fears when dealing with drug addicts. I have had friends have to go on the thirty-day drug cocktail due to needle contamination, and it was not a pleasant experience.

Depending on the drug and/or the chemical components used to make the drug you need to take biohazard precautions into consideration. Many drugs can be ingested through the skin on contact alone. That's why it's important to be aware of the drugs that are popular in your area. In the areas in which I work, PCP is a very popular drug. I know that when I am handling PCP, I need to be extremely vigilant. PCP can be absorbed through contact with the skin. I have had a few friends get contaminated, and it was not pleasant. Not only did they have to be stripped naked and decontaminated in pop-up shower tents; they experienced the effects of the drugs including temperature fluctuations, nausea, and hallucinations. Be aware and take precautions when you're searching individuals you believe can have drugs with these properties.

Recognizing the paraphernalia associated with the popular drugs in your area will help you during your stops. Every drugs needs to be ingested so become familiar with the different modes of ingestion and the paraphernalia they'll need to ingest them. If you're speaking or searching individuals and you start to come across burning caps (little metal melting caps with burn marks on the bottom) or burnt spoons, you can focus your questioning and searches for drugs like heroin. If you are talking to an individual and you notice some steel wool in their bag or on their person, you can start to direct your questioning toward crack, because they'll use steel wool to pack at the bottom of crack pipes.

If you are searching through a bag and you start to see all kinds of pill bottles, you know you'll have to start inspecting the prescriptions and labels on the bottles. If you suspect someone to have PCP, the most likely form of ingestion will be dipping a cigarette or marijuana joint into a vile that contains the drug. If you are searching someone and you come across a vile with tobacco residue on the interior and brownish fluid, you can suspect that it is PCP. Likewise, if you come across cigarettes that are saturated in liquid, are in the pack but soggy, or are packaged separately from the pack of cigarettes, most commonly in a sandwich bag or bottle, you need consider that they could be saturated in PCP and take the necessary precautions. This also applies to knowing which drugs go with other drugs. For example, if you're talking to an individual, and they mention they are on methadone, you know that they have an opiate addiction. You can start to focus your questioning on heroin or prescription opiates. If the individual tells you they are on suboxone, it is used to block opiate uptake receptors in your body so you know to focus your questioning on heroin. I've run across a few DUIs where the individual is on antabuse, which is used for people that have alcohol addictions.

There are too many drugs to list here, but as you get out on patrol, learn the different drugs, paraphernalia, and characteristics associated with those drugs. We talked about paying attention during your stops so pay attention and look for these factors. It'll allow you to customize your questioning during drug stops and also allow you to keep in mind the safety considerations with those drugs.

Remember Your Gloves!

When searching individuals for narcotics, it is critical that you remember to wear your gloves. It is a safety precaution that you can't afford to go without. Make sure that you have at least a pair or two of nitrile or latex gloves on you at all times. As I mentioned, many drugs can be ingested through your skin, and many different types of drug paraphernalia can pose cutting or poking risks. You need to be protected against those risks. When selecting regular search gloves, make sure you select a pair that will still allow you to maintain some dexterity. The last thing you need is for your gloves to be too thick for you to feel anything. It's easy to feel a gun when searching an individual; it's a little harder feeling a bag of heroin.

Physical Characteristics

One of the easiest methods in which to determine if an individual has used drugs are the physical characteristics that they may be displaying. Recognizing these physical characteristics will enable you to better tailor your questions toward detecting if the individual is in possession of drugs. It's reasonable to assume that if the individual has used drugs prior to you stopping them that they may be in possession of drugs while you are stopping them.

Each drug has some different characteristics associated with them; however, most people can recognize when an individual is under the influence of drugs. Perhaps the most obvious sign of drug use is the condition of the eyes. Some of the signs of drug use the eyes could display are being watery and bloodshot, pupils being dilated or contracted, and pupils not responding to stimuli from light sources.

Some drugs will have obvious physical effects and leave telltale signs of use on the user. Heroin addicts will often have track marks appearing on their arms or legs. These are marks from repeated needle use. They may look like swollen bug bites and will typically be found around the forearms of the person. Heroin users will usually have swollen hands and fingers. The swollen hands will be very obvious and will appear to be almost as though they are double in size because they will be filled with so much fluid. Heroin users might also have what is referred to as the "heroin nod." They usually present this when sitting. It'll look as if their head is slowly nodding down toward their stomach. They might have drool coming from their mouth. They will typically be unresponsive, and their eyes will not be responsive to stimuli. Crack cocaine users will often have callous, burnt hands. This will be especially prevalent on their thumbs. You will notice thick calluses there that will appear as though they are slightly black in color. This is from constantly being burned from the heat source they typically use to heat their crack pipes. They may also have burn marks around their lips from the heat of the pipe while smoking it. Crack addicts may appear to be gaunt in the body and face.

Crystal methamphetamine users will also have a gaunt appearance in the face. Crystal meth users will frequently be very paranoid and may become very violent when they're being approached. I have noticed their eyes will be very wild in nature, constantly swinging from side to side. If you happen to come in contact with a PCP user aside from the odor, which we will cover shortly, their eyes will also not be responsive to light. They may start discussing how hot, temperature wise, they feel and may even start to disrobe to the point of being naked. They, too, can become very violent and can even appear as though they're impervious to pain. Their speech may present in a manner consistent with loose association that you will see in psychiatric patients where they will transition between different subject matter in each sentence, none of which will be consistent with each other. Users of prescription drugs will typically have physical symptoms present in their eyes and will typically appear more mellowed out, depending on the drug. Users of designer or club drugs will typical appear a little more "peppy" and upbeat. They, too, may complain of feeling their body temperature rising and become very overheated. A relatively newer drug that is starting to gain popularity is synthetic marijuana, which can be known under many street names but is sold under the label of "potpourri." Since there are so many different kinds of this drug available the physical characteristics that I've observed are far-ranging. The most frequent observations have been eyes that don't respond to light, a sweet odor that isn't similar to marijuana, "zombie"-like behavior where the individual is not aware of their surroundings and possibly even has hallucinations. Some of the individuals I have run across were violent, others more catatonic.

There are an infinite amount of drugs each with some shared characteristics and each with some different characteristics. Learn which drugs are prevalent in your area and start to pay attention to some of the physical characteristics of each. Observing and recognizing these characteristics will help you to tailor your stops and your questioning and will lead to more drug arrests.

Follow Your Nose

In addition to the physical characteristics of drugs, some drugs emit a certain odor that will make them easily identifiable. Recognizing and localizing these odors can, in some cases, lead to the establishment of probable cause and enable a warrantless search of the individual. When establishing an odor emanating from a person, it is important to localize the odor to the person it is coming from unequivocally. In the case of marijuana, if you can localize the odor of marijuana to a particular person, you have probable cause to search that person without a warrant.

Now I want to caution you when it comes to marijuana laws because they have been changing recently. It's important that you're familiar with the marijuana laws in your area. Some of what I am saying could have been changed with the recent legalization of marijuana in a few states. Always follow and remain cognizant of the laws in your areas. If you've stopped, searched, found contraband, and arrested a person based on the localization of the odor of marijuana to their person, this will be the first thing a defense attorney will challenge in court. They'll immediately seek to "prove" that you didn't localize the odor of marijuana to their client. To help mitigate this when reasonable, make sure you can establish the odor of marijuana on their person in as many ways as possible. I will try and establish the odor on them in a few different areas. For example, if they pass by me, I might try and get in position ahead of them at some point and let them pass me again. I might follow them into an area that has different circumstances so that the only things that were consistent to the two areas were me, the defendant, and the odor of marijuana. If you're following them, make sure you state that the odor remained consistent during the duration you were following them for. As you get closer to the individual, if the odor becomes stronger, make sure you state it in your report that as you approached them, the odor grew stronger. Make sure that if there are multiple people in between you and the individual you suspect to have the odor emanating from them, you create an environment where you are able get close enough to the person where there is no doubt in your mind where the odor is coming from. Like I said, you want the only three factors that are always consistent in any circumstance to be—you, the defendant, and the odor of marijuana. Once you can definitively localize the odor, you can conduct the stop.

Once I stop the individual, I will try to establish that they have used the drug on the date I'm stopping them by using a technique that you can employ in almost any stop but especially in drug stops and especially on stops that I have used "plain smell." I'll always try and get the person to admit to me that they have used whatever drug I suspect them to be in possession of on that day. I do this for a variety of reasons. For one, if I can get them to admit to using it that day, especially in the case of marijuana, it will not be hard to explain that if they've used the drug on that day, that they may have the odor of that drug emanating from their person. The second reason is because if they admit to using it that day, it is reasonable to assume that they might be in possession of additional quantities of that drug. The third reason, this is a technique that can be used in the investigation of other crimes as well is that most people will admit to committing smaller offenses rather than admit to committing larger offenses. You can use this admission to the smaller crime to help you tailor your questioning to get them to admit to the larger crimes. You could use this method during questioning and convince the individual that you're there to help them with their addiction. That this could be the first start of getting the help they need to overcome their addiction. Everyone needs to start somewhere, and you're there right now to get him or her started on their recovery and beat the addiction. Like we talked about earlier, compassion will be a much more useful tool during questioning than aggressiveness. If the person doesn't want to admit that they have used the drug, I have found it very successful to get them to admit that they have been around someone else that was using the drug and that perhaps they are just the victim of cross contamination. During the stop, make mental notes of any incriminating statements that indicate drug use or possession and include them in your report.

Marijuana is not the only drug that has a particular odor associated with it. Many different drugs have distinguishing odors associated with them, which can be used as probable cause to search a person. Other drugs such as PCP and methamphetamine also have distinct odors that have been recognized by the courts as establishing probable cause for a search. You'll have to review the laws in your areas to determine if you can establish probable cause for a warrantless search based on the odor of the drug. PCP has distinct odor that you will immediately recognize as having no place on a person. It smells like a very harsh chemical odor, similar to ether. You might smell it on the person's breath, and it might be strong enough to cause you to have to reaction in the form of eye or lung irritation. If you smell PCP on a person, be very cautious and call for backup immediately. Synthetic marijuana has a recognizable sweet aroma. While you might not be able to establish probable cause for a search based on the odor of synthetic marijuana, yet at least it can rise to the level of reasonable suspicion and allow you to stop the individual for further investigation.

Decoy Bags: But It's just a Little

The use of decoy bags is a tactic that drug users and sellers may employ when they're attempting to throw an officer off. Typically, when they're stopped, if they do admit to being in possession of any drugs, they'll retrieve the smallest baggie of drugs you have ever seen. It'll only contain residue or a minuscule amount of the drug. The individual is hoping to play to the fact that if they can convince you that the amount of drugs they possess are so small that you will not even bother with them. They're hoping that you deem the quantity of drugs as too "petty" for you to go any further with the investigation and you'll cut them loose without any further search or action. Don't fall for this trick. If they admit to being in possession of drugs, no matter the quantity, you can search them from head to toe without a search warrant. Make sure you take advantage of this. Explain to them that you understand; however, they will be searched completely. When you are searching them, keep in mind that regardless of what you find and how quick you find it, you still need to search their entire person. If you are searching them and find drugs in the first pocket, don't stop searching. Continue to search their entire body. Most drug dealers may have narcotics on several different parts of their body. They do this in hopes that if they get robbed, someone will not steal all their drugs and for the purpose similar to the decoy bag. If the police stop them and the police only search the first pocket and find the decoy bag, they will stop and cut them loose without further action.

Everyone Starts Somewhere

When testifying during a drug case, the training and experience of the officer will weigh heavily on the opinion of the court. If you're a new officer and it's your first time testifying in court, don't get tripped up or take it personally when a defense lawyer tries to point out that you don't have a lot of experience with drug stops. No matter what, everyone's experience in a certain field starts with the first time. Do not feel ashamed to admit you don't have extensive experience. Testify to what you do have in terms of training and any other legitimate exposure to the drug. As you make more stops, more arrests, and gain more exposure with the drug, you will be able to testify to more experience.

Hands Off!

As you start to make drug arrests and weapons arrests, you will experience a phenomenon in the police world that happens to every police officer. Everyone that shows up on your scene will want to be nosey and handle your evidence. This is especially evident in drug stops. Stand your ground and resist the urge to give in. When recovering drugs, make sure you keep the persons that handle them to a minimum. Resist the urge to pass them around to all the nosey onlookers. Secure them immediately in your pocket or cruiser. Relinquish possession only for investigative purposes such as field tests. After crime scene has processed your drugs, regain possession and take the appropriate action for processing seized drug evidence in your department. Sometimes we're our own worst enemies. The last thing we need is for some kind of chain of custody issue to cost us a conviction. I've said it many times; defense attorneys will attack whatever they can. Don't make it easy for them by having too many hands in the cookie jar.

Slippery Slope

I want to highlight one of my experiences that will draw together a few of the lessons we have been talking about in this section.

It was a very frigid winter night. It was a clear, and the air had that cold bite to it that chilled you right down to the bones. The part of town we were in was a high drug area. I was with two officers whom I work extensively with. We were on foot patrol, and we passed by an individual that was seated. As soon as we passed by him, we recognized the odor of marijuana emanating from his person. We all stopped, made sure that we all had the same observation and decided to pass by the individual again just to verify the odor. We passed by him the second time and again recognized the odor of marijuana emanating from his person. We decided we were going to stop the individual and approached him. He was wearing a heavy winter coat and had a backpack on. My partner started to question him. He admitted to smoking marijuana earlier in the day and stated that was why he smelled of the odor. When my partner asked him if he had any drugs on his person, he stated yes and removed from his coin pocket a small baggie that had a few seeds of marijuana in it. My partner didn't take the bait and started to position the individual for a search. Just then, the individual decided he was going to attempt to flee. We were outside and the ground we were on consisted of tile. It was late at night and frost had settled in on the tile, making it very slick. As the individual took off, my two partners ran after him. The individual took about ten steps and then slipped, falling to the ground. The first officer also slipped failing to the ground, and the second officer slipped over the first and also fell to the ground. It was mildly assuming and the three of them looked like new puppies in a box, each trying to climb over the other, fighting for position. Having the ability for a little hindsight as soon as they slipped onto the ground, I cautiously tiptoed over to the group. I was able to capture the individual and restrain him until my partners gained their bearings and handcuffed him.

During the search of him, we recovered additional marijuana in four separate pockets. We also recovered multiple wads of money from several different pockets as well as a scale. In total we recovered about $1,700 and four ounces of marijuana from the individual. We determined he was lying about his name and discovered that he had open warrants for probation violations stemming from multiple arrests for distribution of narcotics.

From physical characteristics of drug users, plain smell, decoy baggies, recognition of paraphernalia, and special searching considerations, drug stops offer a few different wrinkles that we need to be aware of. As long as you observe and pay attention to these behaviors, you can use these indicators and tips to better craft your stops.

CHAPTER
8

Foot Pursuits

So you've gotten a lookout for a robbery suspect. You're canvassing the area and you spot an individual matching the lookout walking down the street. You pull your cruiser to the side of the road, get out, and start approaching the individual. It's obvious he spots you out of the corner of his eye, and he starts walking at a very brisk pace. You call out, "Police stop!"—all the while picking up the pace you're walking in order to close the distance between the two of you. Again you can tell he can see you because he glances out of the corner his eye, but he still pretends he can't hear you. You start a slow jog to apprehend him, and just like that, he takes off. The race is on...

Before we catch our bad guy, let's stop and identify a few techniques and methods that we can use to avoid a foot race with our individual.

Watch That Body

We're going to focus on the body language signs that could indicate that flight is imminent. Each part of the body has some unique indicators that can be associated with fleeing. As with all body language indicators, the mere presence of any individual indicator does not necessarily mean the corresponding behavior will occur; however, in our line of work, these indicators mean that the likelihood the behavior will occur increases exponentially.

Watch the eyes. This one is pretty simple. Typically where the eyes are looking, the body wants to go. If you have someone stopped and you're talking with him or her and they are staring off in the distance or looking from side to side, you might want to take notice. Now this type of eye movement can also be associated with lying; however, when a suspect intends to flee in will be a more inquisitorial look. The suspect might be staring right through you. This will present as if he looks like he's in a trance. Keep this in mind especially if behind you is an avenue for escape. I've also seen this present as the eyes darting back and forth wildly. Usually the suspect is panicked and will be rapidly sorting through the available options in his head.

Watch the head. This one follows closely with the eyes. By turning their head, the suspect can mitigate moving his eyes. While it is a different technique, the end result is the same. The suspect is scouting the area, looking for an available escape option.

You Can Run but You Can't Hide Forever

I was at one of our local metro stations. It was the middle of rush hour, and the station was relatively busy. I saw the suspect approach the kiosk area where the station attendant was housed. The suspect started to walk toward the station attendant as if he was going to speak with her. He then veered to his left and exited out of the unpaid emergency gate located next to the kiosk. I approached him and asked him what was going on, and he replied that he did not feel that it was necessary to pay for his train ride. I asked for his identification. He handed me his state ID card. I positioned him in the corner of a phone booth and the wall where I thought I could achieve maximum security. The metro stations are always busy and have a large number of individuals moving through them making it a little tougher to find areas that are perfectly conducive to conduct a person stop. Nevertheless, as I was running his information through our communications division, I noticed he kept looking over my shoulder. At the time, I didn't pay it much mind and thought it was kind of strange. As I continued to talk to him, he still kept looking at the ground and kind of turned his head to the right. Just then, the communications division had notified me over the radio that he was 10-75 (the 10 code meaning he had an active warrant). As soon as he heard that phrase, he cut to his right and started to flee. I was able to quickly grab him by the shoulders, and we began grappling, each of us fighting for leverage. At that point, I steered him toward the corner of the phone booth and attempted to get him to the wall to gain some leverage on him. Much to my surprise, when I pushed him into the corner of the phone booth and the wall, he squirted behind the phone booth. Unbeknownst to me, there was a twelve-inch gap between the phone booth and the wall. When I pushed him into the corner, I pushed him into that crevice. I tried to reacquire him; however, the space behind the phone booth was too small for me to fit through. I maintained a grip on him until he violently jerked away further into the gap. At that point, I heard a sickening tearing noise. I looked down at my arm just to realize that my shoulder dislocated out of its socket. It remained dislocated for the next ten minutes or so. Being unable to grip him any further, he made his way out of the other side of the gap and fled. My partner at the time gave chase; however, he lost him in a wooded tree line. I would remain out for eight months and had to have reconstructive surgery on my shoulder. Since I had his identification in my possession, my partner went and swore out a warrant for his arrest. The law eventually caught up with him approximately a year or so later. He was picked up during an armed robbery.

Now could all of this have been prevented? We'll never know; however, could better attention to the details of what his body language was telling me have assisted me? Of course it could have. The eyes are a great indicator of flight. They will usually telegraph where the body will go. Pay attention, and if the suspect displays some of these signs, take the appropriate corrective action (which we will cover at the end).

Happy Feet

Just as important as the watching the eyes, is watching the feet. If the eyes are looking where you want to go, it's the feet that will take them there. Specifically look at the positioning of the feet. Most people, when standing, have their feet shoulder-width apart with their feet slightly turned toward their shoulders. Now I recognize that there is a large disparity in the way people will stand, but once you know what to look for, the feet positioning will become obvious to you.

Now remember when I said the feet will take you where you want to go? As the brain processes where it wants, your feet to go you will notice the toes will slowly start to shift toward the preferred direction of travel. This is the same phenomenon that occurs in bars across the world. Next time you go into your favorite watering hole, look to see if you can find a guy talking to a girl. If he's interested (and he's a guy so he almost certainly will be), take notice of his feet. Most likely, his toes will be pointed at the direction of the girl. It's our brain's way of telling our body what we want. The same behavior will present itself during a subject stop. If you're speaking with the subject and you notice that their toes start to point away from you, you might want to be cognizant of what's in that direction and begin to take corrective action.

While we are on the topic of feet, another popular movement you will observe as a precursor to flight is what I call the hot potato. This is when the suspect, if standing, will begin to almost hop from side to side. The behavior can also be explained as the shifting of weight from side to side. Ever see the beginning of a hockey game when the players are all lined up on the blue line for the national anthem? Each player is shifting the weight of his body from one foot to the other. It presents the same exact way. It's the body preparing to flee.

The shifting of body weight from side to side could also present in another manner. This weight transfer usually occurs right before a suspect is about to be placed in handcuffs. As you grab his hands or arms, you will notice they'll be very tense and rigid. Now it's typical for a suspect to be nervous or tense when being arrested. The difference will be that this amount of rigidness before preparing to flee will be almost to the point where the limbs will be locked in place. Usually the moment the suspect will flee, he will transfer weight to the side of the body that's in the direction he intends to flee. You will notice this especially in the shoulders. The shoulder may dip far lower than the other shoulder. When this dipping motion occurs, they'll most likely flee in the direction of the "dipped" shoulder. We can explain this dip almost like a sprinter's pose. Where the runner dips and prepares their body by getting in the best possible position to run.

It's Too Hot for This

It was a hot summer night, and we were in an area of town that was mostly affluent; however, there was a two- to three-block government-subsidized housing smack dab in the middle of this neighborhood. It literally went from $600,000 homes on one block to the projects right across the street. My partner and I decided that we wanted to monitor that particular neighbor for narcotics activity. We selected an unmarked cruiser and were specifically looking for vehicles that had out of state license plates. After about forty-five minutes or so, a green Ford pulled in front of us. It was a late model, four-door with three occupants. It had a burnt-out rear, passenger-running lamp. We activated our emergency equipment and the vehicle pulled over immediately, just parallel to the first row of subsidized housing. As we were running the license plate of the vehicle, we noticed that the passenger was making a lot of furtive gestures in the area between the center console and the passenger side seat, about right where the passenger side seatbelt would buckle. We took note of that and approached the vehicle.

In the vehicle, there was an older gentleman in the driver side seat who was approximately forty years old and rather obese. In the passenger side seat was a younger kid about sixteen years old with a slim build. He was wearing a white tank top with soccer shorts. In the rear of the vehicle was a young woman about nineteen, also slender. As my partner got information from the driver, I engaged the male passenger in conversation. I obtained his ID and had him step out of the car. His clothes were rather form-fitting, and it was clear he did not have a weapon. However, I still gave him a quick frisk and asked him to be seated on the curb. Instead of sitting down, he just stood still, and I could slowly see his feet start turning in the direction of the housing projects. I immediately lunged to grab him, and it was on. He took off through the housing projects and into the courtyard area of the projects, which much to my chagrin was basically a maze of buildings, backyards, and clotheslines. I was completely surprised by this. As I was chasing him, I started working the radio, giving a description and direction of travel. As I passed by a road sign, I looked up and hastily shouted the street name over the radio. It was one of those things that your eyes process and your mouth says but you really didn't comprehend the word. Just then, communications asked for me to again repeat the street name. I looked up again to ascertain the street name, and when I looked back in front of me, the suspect had taken a turn into another part of the complex. As I approached that turn, I noticed that there were multiple additional directions that he could have fled in. Knowing my partner was still down the block with the two other individuals, I gave up on the pursuit and returned to the vehicle. I was sweating so profusely it looked like I just got out of the shower. We interviewed the driver and passenger then processed the car. In the area where the suspect had been motioning to, we discovered narcotics and some packaging material. A quick interview of the driver revealed that it was basically a mobile drug deal. Warrants were sworn out for his arrest since I still had his ID. He was apprehended a few months later. Once again, the body language screamed he was going to flee. Although I picked up on it a little quicker this time, I was too late.

While not foolproof correctly identifying some of these body language indicators could save you a lot of energy and lead to a safer stop for all involved.

I Can't Hear You . . .

Now getting back to our original scenario where the robbery suspect is now running away from you. You will be presented with this type of runner quite frequently regarding lookouts. This type just pretends he doesn't hear you. He knows you are talking to him by the nervous glances over the shoulder; however, he pretends he can't hear you. In this scenario, the inevitable result is that he is about to flee. The only thing you can do is close the distance between the two of you quick enough that you startle him and are able to apprehend him before he fully takes off.

Before you think that all I do is get beat at foot pursuits, let me share a story about the "if I ignore him, it's not me" fleers. It was late on a Friday night, and I was just about headed to check off when I noticed a kid causing some trouble in one of the underground portions of the city. The individual was a tall, goony, preppy-looking, college-aged kid. As we began to walk toward him, he saw us out of the corner of his eye and started to walk faster. I called out to the group of friends he was with, and they simply played stupid and pretended I wasn't talking to them even though they were the only ones around. As I got a little closer, he picked up his pace until eventually he was a in a full-out sprint. As we ascended an escalator outside, I was immediately overwhelmed with the super charged frigid air that had ascended on the area. We're talking single digits and anyone that runs in the cold knows it is miserable.

As he cleared to corner of a large office building, I lost sight of him. I stopped and looked around for a few seconds and noticed that he had hid behind the corner of a building down the block. I continued to chase him until we eventually ran in a circle. By about the fifth block, my lungs started to burn due to the air and exertion level. I could see the suspect, but I started to lose ground. I noticed an older guy getting into a Range Rover and approached him. I asked him if he could give me a quick ride up the block and pointed toward the suspect. He hesitated for a minute and stated he was had to pick up his wife. I leaned on him a little more, and he obliged. I hopped in the passenger side, he pulled a U-turn, and he dropped me off right in front of a bus stand where the suspect had run into and took a seat, hoping that for whatever reason I might forget that it was him. I rushed over and apprehended him without a struggle. As backup arrived and I handed him off, I almost collapsed because my lungs were just on fire. That entire weekend, I could barely breath, but luckily, I suffered no lasting effects.

Safety First!

While nothing can be more fun and get your adrenaline pumping faster than a foot pursuit can there are some practical and officer safety considerations that need to be addressed when you are considering engaging in a foot pursuit.

While it is important why the suspect decided to flee, it should not be a deciding factor as to whether you should pursue or not. In my experience, about 85 percent of the times, a suspect fled from me in was for a specific reason. Sometimes they were in possession of narcotics, other times they had active warrants against them, and other times they matched a lookout. After you catch them, you'll have more than enough time to figure out the why. I have caught the other 15 percent of suspects, and after catching them, all excited that I was about to recover untold numbers of narcotics, I was disappointed to learn they just ran because they were scared. This will happen. You will put in all that legwork only to learn that there was no real reason they ran in the first place. Don't fret about it; you still did good work. The suspect knows why he or she is fleeing, and unless you are a psychic, you will not. Your objective is to capture that individual in as safe a way as possible, ensuring both you and the suspect remain as unharmed as the circumstances permit. If you can identify a certain crime or know why they are fleeing, go ahead and include that information with your radio transmission, but again, keep in mind only they know why they are fleeing. You might think it's shoplifting, but they know they have a handgun in their waistband. From the shoplifting to murder, you should treat the pursuit as serious as possible.

Roger, Roger!

Use your radio. During a foot pursuit, this is especially important. You need to make your communications division and other officers in the area aware that you are in a foot pursuit and you require additional assistance. You don't know how long or where the pursuit will bring you, so it is crucial for other officers to get a head start responding to your position. Among the first transmissions you should put out should be a subject description. I know you'll be running around, equipment flapping all over the place, but take the few seconds it takes to put out a quick flash lookout. Aside from the usual information, which we already covered, try and include something unique to that particular suspect. Do they have a certain type and style of shoe? Do they have clothing items with certain easily recognizable logos? Do they have particular tattoos? Are they shirtless? The more specific the information is, the better. You never know what other officers will be in the area.

The more specific the lookout is, the easier it can be for other officers to identify that individual and capture them. Included in the description should be whether or not the suspect is armed, and if so, with what. If you know for sure they are armed, give a description of the weapon. If you aren't sure if they are armed, you can simply state that it is unknown. Regardless, treat every fleeing suspect as if they are armed and proceed with extreme caution.

Which Way Did He Go?

Just as crucial as the description of the individual is the direction they are fleeing in. Most of us work and are familiar with the areas we patrol. Make sure to include the actual direction of travel (if known), the street or highway name, and any prominent landmarks. It's easy during a pursuit to get mixed up with are we running north, south, east, or west so including popular landmarks will greatly assist additional units that are arriving to the area. Most people may not know what travelling north on whatever street may be, but stating a landmark such as a popular corner store, tourist attraction, or restaurant will help responding officer immediately visualize were you are. Keep in mind to offer updated locations throughout the pursuit as many times as practical. Remember responding officers need to get to your exact position, not the position you were at even one minute ago. Seconds matter when it comes to officer safety. You need to keep the responding units as informed as possible.

Butter Fingers?

When you're running, you will lose equipment, so be prepared. It's a forgone conclusion that some piece of equipment will become dislodged and fall to the ground; don't freak out. Know in your mind what you can afford to lose and what you should recover. You can manage without your citation clipboard, but should you continue to pursue if you drop your magazines? Regardless of what you drop, do your best to put it over the radio so subsequent units may be able to retrieve it. I personally have dropped many items from the aforementioned clipboard to an asp baton.

I've heard other officers radioing that they have dropped magazines. The decision of terminating the pursuit due to lost equipment will be subjective and up to each officer to decide. Keep in mind, however, if you drop something, you should be prepared to lose it. There's no guarantee that you'll recover that item. So along with practical considerations, safety considerations need to be considered. You don't need crucial pieces of your equipment falling into the hands of bad guys or in the hands of some innocent kids playing in the yard. The same can be said if you see the suspect discarding something. In that case, advise over the radio where an item was discarded and if possible what it could be. This will ensure responding units could recover possible evidence that will be important to your case. Start considering now what you can afford to lose and what you can't so by the time you get in that first pursuit, you can focus on the important parts.

Be Aware of Your Surroundings

It's a miracle for me to have watched suspects dart into a heavily travelled street bustling with activity and remain unscathed. This phenomenon seems only to occur in the benefit of the suspect. They'll have no problems whereas you will step one foot off the curb and hear nothing but screeching brakes and blaring horns. Exercise extreme caution while crossing streets, highways, train tracks, tunnels, and any other area in which motorists or individuals operating equipment aren't expecting a human being to be. Safety should be a primary concern at all times.

If You Need It, Ask for It

It's never a bad idea to ask for additional resources that could assist you during your foot pursuit. If you have patrol K-9's available for your use ask for one to respond. They can assist you with the apprehension of the individual, the backtracking for evidence, and the setting up of a perimeter. If you have access to a helicopter, ask. It's not your responsibly to authorize the use of a helicopter, but asking never hurt anyone. I'm sure that the pilots will be more than willing to put their equipment and skills to use. If you have specialized equipment, such as night-vision goggles or thermal imagers, that can help you search wooded areas get them to the scene. Only you know what resources you have available to you in your department. Don't be afraid to ask and put those resources to use catching your bad guy.

Know When to End It

Even though you want to catch your suspect, it's important to know when you should terminate a foot pursuit.

Are you solo? If so, how far away is backup? Obviously, your goal is to end the pursuit as quickly as possible, but the longer it continues, the more safety considerations that need to be accounted for. If you're solo, how much energy are you willing to exert to capture the suspect? How much energy will you expect to have if he continues to fight you after you catch him? These are questions only you can answer. Physical endurance will play a large role in your ability to resolve the pursuit in as safe a manner as possible. The last thing you want to do is capture the suspect but not have enough energy to actively engage a resisting suspect. This is an extremely unsafe situation that could have life-or-death consequences associated with it. If you feel yourself becoming too exhausted to continue, communicate over the radio that you're terminating the pursuit and include the last known direction of travel. We're not superman. There's no shame in terminating a pursuit because of fatigue. In most cases, we're carrying upwards of thirty pounds of equipment, so it already isn't a fair fight. You might get a little teasing, but you can't afford to let your ego get the best of you; too much is at stake.

In a pursuit, your radio is your lifeline. If you lose your ability to communicate using your radio, terminate the pursuit immediately. Losing the ability to communicate puts you in a precarious situation that's highly unsafe. You will no longer be able to offer position updates, ensuring your backup will have to guess at where you are. You'll lose the ability to communicate changes in the suspect such as clothing changes or if the suspect suddenly presents a weapon or even if another party gets involved to aid the suspect. A foot pursuit is a fluid circumstance that can constantly change. New challenges will constantly be presenting themselves to you. Your ability to provide real-time information is crucial to safety, and there's little to no reason to continue a pursuit if your ability to communicate is compromised.

If you become injured in any way, terminate the pursuit immediately. Indicate over the radio the extent of your injury and the last known location of the suspect. Depending on your injury, either get into a defensive posture or make your way out to the nearest landmark or thoroughfare and wait for backup to arrive. Physical confrontations with suspects aren't the only ways in which you can be injured. Just like in any sport, non-contact injuries can occur at any time. These can include sprains, broken bones, ligament injuries, or the like. Running especially with all that extra weight over uneven terrain will cause injury. Be cognizant of that and proceed with caution. You are no good to anyone if you capture the suspect but are too injured a successfully handcuff and arrest them.

If you lose sight of the suspect for an extended period of time, or the suspect enters a residence, building, or wooded area that can be reasonably secured, end the pursuit and focus on setting up a perimeter. There's no need to enter a residence that you're unfamiliar with. You have no reason to know why the suspect selected that residence. He could know it, and he could have reinforcements in the way of additional persons or weapons lying in wait. It's dangerous to go barging into an unknown environment when you could simply summon additional resources, set up a perimeter, and resolve the situation in another manner.

Now if they present additional threats to the occupants of the home or building in the way of immediate physical harm to the residents, you might have no choice but to enter. But in the absence of immediate physical harm to the occupants, it's better to set up a perimeter and wait for additional resources. The same can be said if you end up losing sight of the suspect. You don't need to be going on a fishing expedition through unknown neighborhoods or areas. If you lose sight of the suspect, you never know where he could spring up. He could be lying in, waiting around a corner, under a car, in a house, or wherever. Under extreme circumstances, he could even be leading you into an ambush. The last thing you need to be doing is wandering around. If you get lost or are no longer able to intelligibly communicate your position to responding officers, terminate the pursuit. If no one knows where you are, all the resources you have available to you are useless. In some of the areas in DC, we've even encountered street signs that have been purposely changed to confuse responding police officers. Getting lost is dangerous. The number of safety concerns in any of these scenarios could be endless. If you lose sight of the subject, communicate his last known location and start to set up you perimeter. Maintain pursuit discipline and terminate the pursuit if necessary.

Got 'Em!

You caught them! Good job! You are a perfect physical specimen. The suspect thought he could get the better of you but little did he know you were a first team all- American track star. Now what?

Get the handcuffs on as quickly as possible. The quicker you handcuff the suspect, the less likely it is that you will be drawn into a physical altercation, which is especially important due to the amount of effort you have already expended. Once the suspect is handcuffed, let your communications division know you've apprehended the suspect, if there are any injuries, and your location. Remember once the handcuffs are on, it's over. Don't let your emotions get the better of you. Use the appropriate amount of force that's necessary (keeping in mind it might not take any force; they could simply give up) to affect the arrest. If the area in which you executed the arrest in has the potential to be unsafe, like the middle of an unfriendly housing complex, try to move the suspect to the nearest roadway or landmark if possible. Keep in mind it could take a while for back up to locate you off the beaten path somewhere. If it's safe and reasonable, advise over the radio you'll be moving the suspect to an easily recognizable location, ensuring backup can arrive and locate you quicker.

Get your breathing under control. If other units are on scene, allow them to watch your suspect and take a few minutes to get your breathing under control. Once you have settled down, do a quick inventory of yourself. Make sure you are not injured and ascertain whether or not you have lost any equipment along the way. If you have lost equipment, advise your supervisor as soon as possible.

Backtrack

Perhaps one of the most overlooked post pursuit activities is to always backtrack the route in which you have travelled, within reason. It's difficult during the course of the pursuit to monitor every movement that the suspect makes. Oftentimes, they could discard or hide evidence unbeknownst to you. It's important that you thoroughly examine the route in which you ran for possible evidence. Take as much time as you need doing this. Don't let other officers or supervisors rush the search. Oftentimes, additional evidence recovered during this search will be important to your case. Keep in mind that if you didn't see them discard the evidence, you still need to obtain some other evidence that ties the suspect to the contraband such as a statement, fingerprints, etc.

I can recall one particular arrest in which this was especially helpful. It was the middle of the week and my partner and I were on foot patrol. It was mid-afternoon and it was a nice, cool fall day with a slight breeze. My partner and I were monitoring a bus stop for signs of general disorder. My partner noticed an individual that was giving one of the bus drivers a hard time, so we decided to approach the individual. He was a young man, early twenties, slim build, and pretty tall. He was wearing a tank top and shorts, perfect fleeing attire. As my partner was talking to him, he started to display some of the body language indicators we've been talking about. He wasn't looking at my partner but instead was looking "through" him. His feet slowly started to shift away from us toward the opening of a parking garage. Behind the suspect was a six-foot-high fence and behind us, in the direction the suspect was looking, was the opening to a parking garage. On the other side of the parking garage was a small street that connected to a neighborhood of single-family homes. The conversation only lasted for a few seconds when the suspect started to blade his body slowly toward where his feet were pointed. Deciphering this behavior, my partner lunged toward the suspect just as he turned to flee. My partner missed, fell to the ground, attempted to get up and subsequently tripped over the curb, landing on the ground again.

Afterward, we had a good laugh about it due to the fact my partner was rolling on the ground and looked like a teen dry humping the pavement. Shaking my partner, the suspect took off into the entrance of the parking garage. I circled around the bus stand we were next to and started to pursue the suspect. We ran through the entrance of the parking garage, and I was only about twenty yards behind the suspect. Lucky for me, the parking garage was rather large, and it was probably around three hundred yards between the entrance of the parking garage and the exit onto the street with a fairly unobstructed view. As we ran through the garage past rows of cars, I was able to gain about ten yards on the suspect. Realizing this, he cut over into the next lane of the garage and started ducking between cars.

Every time he ducked under a car, I lost sight of him for a second or two. Fearing he might draw a weapon, I drew my own weapon out, slowed my pace slightly, and bent my knees slightly to make my figure harder to target. After about the tenth time he ducked, he decided to go for broke and attempted to outsprint me for the last one hundred yards or so. We had already been sprinting for about two hundred yards, so I was fairly fatigued, but that little slow down in the garage gave me a few seconds to rest my legs. The suspect got another thirty yards or so before I caught him right at the exit of the garage. I used a technique that most will advocate in place of tackling, which is to push using both hands on one shoulder of the suspect. This caused him to lose balance, and he stumbled to the ground. My partner finally caught up to us, and we successfully handcuffed him. As we were handcuffing the suspect, he had the strong odor of marijuana emanating from his person; however, a search of the defendant yielded no marijuana.

After we got the suspect searched and into the cruiser, I couldn't figure out why the suspect kept ducking under cars. He gave away a huge advantage by continuously slowing down and ducking behind the cars. An advantage that, on the face of it made no sense. Had he exerted all that effort into running, he may have gotten away. I shared my concerns with my partner, and we decided to thoroughly check the route in which we ran. We took about twenty-five minutes backtracking the route. We got down and checked underneath every car we passed. The search yielded nothing significant. We were just about to give up when just like in the movies, I noticed a glint of light coming from one of the wheel wells of one of the cars the suspect had ducked behind. I went to the wheel well and retrieved from it a softball-sized bag of marijuana. We would later be able to reaffirm that the suspect was in possession of the marijuana during an interview of the suspect.

This goes to show that just because you caught your suspect, it doesn't mean that the hard work is over. Due your case due diligence and be thorough. Backtracking your route could be the difference between a good case and a great one.

End It before It Starts!

While nothing gets your adrenaline pumping and heart racing like a foot pursuit, there are several factors to take into consideration in order to mitigate the chances of a fleeing suspect. It's a much safer outcome when your suspect doesn't flee. You will not be able to prevent this every time, but we'll look at a few strategies you can use to mitigate a foot pursuit.

As with every stop, you should always get the suspect's identification as soon as possible. Now in some circumstances such as receiving a lookout, you will not be able to get the suspect's identification right away, but on most other occasions, you should be able to get your suspect's identification right away. This serves two purposes. The first is that if you have identified the suspect and they know that you have identified them, they're less likely to flee. They may figure since you've already identified them, there is no point in fleeing. The second reason is that if you've gotten their identification and they decide to flee, you already have identified them. Even if they outrun you, you can still go and obtain warrants for their arrest. Now if they get away and ditched some sort of evidence, you will never figure that out but you can still obtain a warrant if they committed a criminal offense when you stopped them and for the fleeing and/or resisting. The few times I've been beat on foot pursuits, I was bailed out by already having the suspect's identification. This ensures that the suspect will be brought to justice, just not as quickly as you would've originally hoped for.

We've spoken a lot about different body language indicators up to this point. The reason being that body language telegraphs a suspect's future moves. Understanding these is important to buying yourself a few extra seconds to make crucial decisions. If you recognize any of the indicators we talked about, you need to take corrective action immediately. If you are solo upon recognition of any of the fleeing indicators, you should immediately request backup. This will ensure that officers start heading to your area in the case of a foot pursuit. Another officer might be right around the corner and could respond before you know it, mitigating the chances that your suspect flees. Radioing for backup might also let your suspect know that more officers will be arriving soon, and they might feel as though it's against their best interests to flee.

If the fleeing body language indicators appear, reposition your suspect. This serves many purposes. The first is that repositioning them changes the dynamics for them. If they intended to flee, they now will have to spend additional time readjusting whatever tactics they came up to suit the new environment. This will buy you more time and could make it harder for them to flee. When repositioning your suspect, put them in a position of disadvantage. Move them to a location where they can sit on the ground. Scout the area around you for items you can use such as a curb or a chair. Having them sit down greatly reduces the chances they will flee. It buys you extra time because if they intend to flee, they would have to rise to their feet. You can take it one step further by having your suspect cross their feet at the ankles while sitting. It'll make it very difficult for them to get into an advantageous position to flee. As you're waiting for backup, keep your suspect talking. You don't want their mind to be on the subject of fleeing. Keeping them engaged in conversation will keep their mind off of fleeing and may buy you the extra time you need for backup to arrive and the scene to become more secure.

Pay attention and stay alert. Being attentive to the suspect will make the suspect question if they'll actually be able to pull off fleeing from you. In their mind, they might even think that you know that they intend to flee. This gives you a powerful psychological advantage. It allows the suspect to start second guessing themselves, buying you extra time.

If you feel as though a flight is imminent, close the gap. Either grab or physically restrain the suspect as soon as possible. Now you don't have to slam them to the ground or tackle them, but a firm grab of the arm can be just fine. This obviously sends a clear message that they aren't going anywhere. You can also have them turn around, move their feet apart, and handcuff them if you feel that flight is imminent.

Before we wrap up, I want to bring your attention to a scenario that arose that encompasses a lot of the factors we've been talking about. The scenario involves a foot pursuit and subsequent shooting that occurred in Muskogee, Oklahoma. The video is available online, and I encourage everybody to take a look at it. In our career, aside from experiencing a lot of these scenarios, it's difficult to get insight into some of these situations. It's helpful to go and watch some of the videos from the officers that were involved in some of these incidents. You can learn through their experiences from both what they did wrong and what they did right. You can envision yourself in their shoes and run yourself through the scenario in your own mind. The incident took place on January 17, 2015.

An officer had been dispatched to a call at a local church for a suspect that had threatened his girlfriend by stating he "had a bullet with your name on it." As the officer approaches the suspect, he is in a church parking lot accompanied by a few other individuals. The officer immediately asked the suspect to take his hands out of his pockets and moves to frisk the individual due to the possibility of him being armed. As the officer makes contact with the individual, he immediately notices that he's very nervous and is shaking. The suspect's arms are rigid to the point that they're entirely erect and are locked at the elbows. As the officer begins to pat him down, you will notice that the suspect's right shoulder drops lower than the left shoulder. The suspect then flees. The officer gives chase and they run out of the parking lot and onto a street. As the chase is unfolding, the suspect drops what appears to be a gun. The suspect then retrieves the gun and, while bent over, turns the gun toward the officer. The officer draws his firearm and fires at the suspect multiple times, striking him three times. The suspect falls to the ground dead.[16]

This scenario personifies a lot of what we discussed. When watching the video, the body language indicators could not have been clearer that flight was imminent. It also shows how the circumstances of a stop and flight could instantly change. The original call was a domestic disturbance. When the suspect fled, the officer really didn't have too much information as to why he was fleeing or any additional criminal charges on the suspect. However, the circumstances of the stop changed drastically when the suspect dropped and then presented the weapon to the officer. The officer had a split second

[16] Ray Sanchez. Oklahoma Police Officer's Body-Cam Captures Fatal Shooting. Posted January 24, 2015. Accessed May 10, 2016. http://www.cnn.com/2015/01/23/us/oklahoma-police-shooting-video/index.html

to process the change in the scenario from domestic disturbance to deadly force encounter. Circumstances can change in an instant in this career and the officer had to improvise in nanoseconds to ensure his safety.

Although nothing can be more fun than foot pursuits, there are many practical and safety considerations that need to be made. Each scene is different and has a different set of circumstances and factors involved. Foot pursuits are a very fluid, dynamic. One size may not fit all. Recognizing early warning signs of fleeing are important and will be helpful to you. The goal of every stop is to leave the stop as safely as you entered it. Recognizing these indicators will ensure that you buy yourself a few extra seconds of reactionary time, ensuring that you can take the best and most appropriate action you can to ensure you remain as safe as you can.

PART

Three

CHAPTER

9

Narrative Writing

We've just dropped our prisoner off at processing, and it's now time for every officer's favorite activity—paperwork! Paperwork in general gets a bad name, but one of my favorite parts of the job is writing the police narrative. The importance of a well-written police narrative cannot be underscored. Of course, the actual grammatical construction of your narrative is important, but we're going to focus more intently on what should be in your narrative. How does it sound to the reader? Supervisors, officers, lawyers, etc., will see your narrative. It's often among the first pieces of information that will be presented for your case. You want anyone that's reading your narrative to know that the person writing it is a serious, smart police officer.

Paint a Picture

You will hear me talk a lot about "painting a picture." We in the police world have a tendency to make our writing robotic, and to me, *robotic* means boring. While we do have to get vital information across to the reader, we often forget that the majority of the people that will read our narratives are not police officers. We need to understand that we have to write for our audience. We were on scene. We know exactly what happened. The reader doesn't, and it's our responsibility to bring them there. We want to write in a manner that transports them from their desk or office directly to the scene of or narrative. We want to engage our reader and present the information so that the reader seems as though they are reading a really good book. We want the narrative to read like a story would read while still getting all the pertinent information across that's to be expected from a police narrative.

Setting the Stage

Among the first item in every police narrative should be the time, place, and location. This begins to set the stage for the reader. Included among this information can be other factors that help set the stage. Try describing the weather conditions, the lighting, type of area, the amount of foot traffic, the landmarks nearby that could help the reader visualize the location, the physical characteristics of the building or area you're in. All this information will allow the reader to set the stage much like when they begin to read a story in their favorite book. It allows them to start transporting themselves to the scene.

While describing the physical conditions of the scene are important, an oft forgotten part of setting the stage involves setting the stage for the emotions, expressions, or actions of the individuals involved. Remember, your narrative is just words on paper. It is not a movie containing visual and audio cues. You need to convey to the reader the emotion of the parties involved. You want the reader to feel the emotions that the actors felt. You want the reader to see the emotions through their own eyes. To have them connect with the writer and help them understand what you were seeing. If you're successful in conveying the emotions, you can help the reader better understand why you took the action you did. Make sure you describe the emotions and actions of the actor. Don't say the individual acted in a combative manner toward you.

While most police officers can probably visualize this, most laypersons may not. You're creating a scenario where the reader will have to be subjective and use his or her own precepts to define what you mean. You don't want this ambiguity seeping through. Instead, be descriptive, specific, and define for the reader what combative looks like. It might sound something like this: "I approached the individual and the first thing that I noticed was that the individual was clearly agitated. His face was flush and the veins on his neck started to protrude out. He was staring intently at me, burning a hole through me with his eyes. His limbs got very tense and rigid. His legs were slightly bent at the knees, and he was rocking on the balls of his feet as if ready to pounce. He brought his arms up to the front of his body, right below his chest, and clenched his fists so tightly that his knuckles began to turn white. He was shouting in a loud and profuse manner, all the while spittle kept forming on the corners of his mouth. He appeared as if was ready to fight me."

Being descriptive in this manner will allow the reader to see and experience what you saw and felt. This leaves the reader with no doubt as to what "combative" means. We don't want any ambiguity in our writing. If you leave gaps or ambiguous language in your narrative, it's the reader that will fill in those gaps with their own interpretation of what they think should be in there. Remember, the reader wasn't there and can't "see" words. Any emotions, expressions, or actions need to be explained in detail. Describe, don't say.

Be Thorough

Over the years, I have written and read many police narratives, and I can tell you for a fact that one of my biggest pet peeves is reading a five-line narrative for a robbery report. The point of the narrative is to convey information. So use it to convey information. Your narrative offers no investigative capital if it lacks the requisite details to be useful. Make sure you're thorough. The goal is to have the reader read through your narrative, and it's so thorough that they ask you little to no follow-up questions. Make sure you include all the case details from witness statements, to show-ups, to your own observations, to any evidence that was recovered. One of the items I will always make sure are included in my narrative is chain of custody information when it comes to seized evidence. Whether it's drugs, weapons, or some other evidence, I will always include in the chain of custody who I found it on and where on the person I found it, what officer found it, which officer if any conducted crime scene on the item, who transported it to the property or evidence office, and who submitted it into property. Even if you have separate chain of custody forms, it doesn't hurt to include that information in the narrative itself. It is much more likely that an additional property/chain of custody report will get lost than your arrest report being lost for good.

Part of being thorough includes having someone else proofread your narrative. No matter how well you write, there will never be any harm done by someone else reviewing your work. We all make mistakes, and we all have a tendency to miss mistakes in our writing because we're reading it as it sounds in our head. We could easily glance over an error or two and not even know it. Getting a second pair of eyes will help with grammatical errors and substantive errors. Proofreading is a part of any good writing process. It deserves to be a part of yours.

He Did What?

When writing your narrative, make sure you explain the elements of whatever crime you have charged them with. Oftentimes, I will try and use the exact wording from the charging document itself in my narrative. This serves two purposes. Some jurisdictions will present the arrest report to a commissioner or magistrate for them to determine what the person's release status will be. You want to make sure that whatever you have charged them with is accurately portrayed and the commissioner or magistrate can understand, review, and make the appropriate decisions in regard to their release status. Stating the charging language in the narrative will allow the attorneys, prosecutor, and defense to quickly conceptualize what charges have been levied against the defendant.

Lastly, using the charging language will help you learn the law. Criminal codes are oftentimes hundreds of pages. Nobody knows them all. We get into the habit of just charging certain crimes that we come across most frequently. We also may take blind advice from other officers on what to charge without first reading the code. If we don't read the code, we may be charging individuals inappropriately. Incorrectly charging the defendant could lead to the charges against them being dismissed. Due your due diligence and read through what you are charging the person with. Make sure all the elements of the crime are met. Once you become an expert in your charges, you can articulate to the prosecutor, defense, and courts why you charged what you did and why the defendant is guilty of those charges.

I Don't Want a Piece of Them

Writing a thorough, well-written, and descriptive report will ensure that your case may never even see the inside of a courtroom. If your report is detailed and paints a clear picture of the defendant's actions that lead to their arrest, a defense attorney might read over it and decide they want no part of the officer that wrote that. You might force the defense attorney into considering a plea in your case because they know the alternative will mean a swift conviction. The better the narrative, the more leverage you give the prosecutor for a plea deal. No ambiguity in your reports means that the amount of possible legal challenges and suppression motions from the defense will be either limited or non-existent, and they'll be more likely to consider a plea. Going to trial is all well and good, but when you go to trial, no matter how strong the case, the outcome can never be guaranteed. Writing a thorough, well-written report will ensure that the majority of your cases will end favorably to the prosecutor.

Being thorough in your report becomes critical when your case gets to court. The defense attorney will fill in any omissions in your report with what benefits them the most. They'll attempt to equate omissions with purposeful deceit or incompetence. This will be harmful to your case and will only allow for the defense attorney to have you backtracking. Instead of focusing on the facts of the case, the defense will spend the majority of your testimony, questioning you as to why your report lacks this or that. They'll then fill in whatever omissions they have found in your report with whatever is most advantageous to them or their client. Many cases go to trial months if not years after the initial arrest. Thorough, well-written reports will allow you to remember in detail the facts surrounding your case. This will allow you to intelligently testify about your case even if you are at trial a year later.

It's not the sexiest part of police work, but it is one of the most important and demands your time and attention. A well-written police narrative will assist you in becoming a better police officer. You will learn to articulate yourself in a way that lets your reader visualize in their mind the scene that you experienced. You'll learn the law and legal codes better by reviewing each charge and explaining them in your narrative. And you will ensure that you give the prosecutor the maximum amount of leverage they need to reach a successful disposition in your case.

CHAPTER

10

Taking the Stand

You just arrested a subject. It's a slam-dunk case and you feel great. You're still riding the high and self-satisfaction of the arrest. Your peers are high-fiving you, your supervisors are commending you. All that training and persistence paid off. The case is over and your subject will have to face the consequences of his actions, right? Wrong. After the initial arrest, you certainly have a lot to be proud of; however, you are only halfway to the finish line. The arrest is only the stage at which you deliver the subject to the justice system. It's now time for the case to be played out in front of the courts.

A crucial function of the duties of a police officer is their ability to appear and testify in court. For testifying is just one piece of the puzzle when it comes to the criminal justice system. It serves the public no good if police are excellent at stopping crime and removing criminals from the street, but they're inept at testifying. This would lead to the very criminals they took of the street to begin with, returning to the streets having little recourse taken against them. Testifying in court is like the follow through on a baseball swing. You still want to focus on gripping the bat, swinging, and making solid contact with the ball; however, to achieve the desired result, you still must follow through with your swing. Testifying can be seen in the same light. You have used excellent police skills to build a case against an individual that lead to an arrest, but you must still follow through by delivering effective testimony and ensuring that the fact finding body whether it be a judge or jury have all the facts that they require to make the most informed decision possible.

Most officers are nervous when the thought of testifying arises and for good measures. Testifying contains many of the greatest fears of humans, including public speaking and the participation in an adversarial forum. Many people, including police officers, not only struggle with public speaking but also have a genuine fear of public speaking. Don't let that get inside your head. Just like anything else testifying is a skill that can be honed over time with practice and experience. Many new officers also have to grapple with the fact that they're now a piece in what's called an adversarial forum. Humans by nature are uncomfortable confronting other humans. We're social by nature and most adhere to the saying that we go along to get along.

We're socialized from an early age to avoid confrontation. Well, as soon as you put that badge on, you have to prepare yourself for the possibility of confrontations, both inside the courtroom and out. You've entered a career where you have awesome power and responsibilities, and as we know from a popular superhero movie, "with great power comes great responsibility." The outcome of our actions and testimony in court can lead to the loss of liberty for an individual (keeping in mind the responsibility for the loss of liberty were the actions the defendant took, not the actions you took). Testifying in court is a serious role and should be treated as such. The importance should not be underscored, as it is an essential function in our criminal justice system.

My First Time . . .

Before we get started, let me share my first experience with testifying in court. It was the summer after I first graduated from the police academy, and I was testifying as a witness in which another officer was the arresting officer. This particular officer was a beast of a man, a real physical freak of nature, tall, fit, shaggy, blond hair, not particularly good-looking, always bearing an inquisitorial look on his face. One day during physical training in the academy, he took us for a run through the neighborhood and into a cemetery. The roads in this particular cemetery wound back and forth in very long stretches all the while going uphill. It wasn't a particularly hot day; however, due to the nature of the terrain in which we were running, it was a pretty grueling run. We started with around ten or so recruits at the start of the run, and after 5.5 miles of running, this officer looks back and sees only me. The look on his face turned from its usual fierce determination to a more quizzical look. He looked at me and asked where everyone else had fallen to. I said I have no idea, I assume they're all spread out over the course of the cemetery, stretched out on the ground. He looks at me, shrugs, and then says, "I'll race you back to training" and promptly sprints off like a gazelle.

This particular officer would never have been confused for a Rhodes scholar, but he made up for it in heart and determination. We were at one of the stations in a depressed part of town. This area was known for crime, general disorder, and an overall lack of disregard and respect when it came to the police. It was early in the afternoon and the kids had just been let out of school. The juvenile activity in this part of the city was heavy. This officer stopped one of the juveniles for a minor offense, and the juvenile decided he was not going to be bothered by this officer, which as is it turns out, was not a good decision by that juvenile. The officer began struggling with the juvenile, and I rushed to help him subdue and secure the juvenile. As they continued to struggle, the officer and I proceeded to do the officer shuffle, a move that happens when two officers are simultaneously trying to get the best position for leverage on the same person. Usually this ends up looking like a weird junior prom dance move because there just isn't enough room to go around. As I'm jockeying for position, the juvenile strikes me with his right hand in the stomach area, but I can barely feel it due to my ballistic vest. As previously mentioned, this officer is a physical freak and ends up slamming both him and me to the ground. We eventually are able to get the juvenile hand-cuffed, and he affects the arrest without any further issues.

A few weeks later, I was called to testify for the first time. I was nervous. I remember not quite being sure what to expect. I reviewed my notes and the arrest report, but there was this feeling that I wasn't quite prepared. We as human beings tend to underestimate the amount of our preparation. No one will hold you to a higher standard than yourself. As I went into the courtroom for the first time, I was slightly overwhelmed. I saw the judge sitting up on his bench, which as typical is raised over the courtroom. To my left was the prosecutor and to my right the defendant and his lawyer. I was sworn in and began my testimony. The prosecutor walked me through his line of questioning and I thought, "Man, this is pretty easy. I'm just about in the clear."

After the prosecutor finished his questioning, it was then the defense's turn to cross-examine me. Let me start by saying that I ended up getting the better of him that day, but my first exposure to cross-examination was an interesting one. The defense attorney went to great lengths attacking the procedures, use of force, and the grappling techniques that were applied. At one point, he even asked me to demonstrate to the court what an arm bar takedown looked like, and I all too happily jumped up and told him to come toward me. Startled, he then, to my severe disappointment, asked me to perform the takedown on myself. Chuckling inside, I attempted to illustrate to the court an arm bar takedown using only myself, which, needless to say, looked look a weird game of solo twister. During my testimony, the defendant kept peering at me, his eyes cutting right through mine in a clear attempt to intimidate me; he was shaking his head back and forth after almost every statement I made. When my testimony concluded, I exited the courtroom and took a seat in the witness waiting area. As I was reflecting in the waiting area and playing the events of the last hour over and over in my head, it was striking to realize that the defense attorney asked me a whole assortment of questions; however, none of them had any relevance to the actual guilt of the defendant. Several hours later, the prosecutor emerged from the double doors of the courtroom and announced that the defendant had been found guilty. For all the preparation and nerves, I felt my first experience testifying paled to comparison to the horror I thought it would be. From that day on, even though I would experience nerves before testifying, I looked forward to performing that duty with an enthusiastic vigor.

Preparation

Prior to your career, the chances are slim that you would have garnered enough experience in courtroom testimony to be considered an expert, but there are several things you can do to prepare yourself for the eventuality of testifying.

As stated in the Art of War, "The general who wins the battle makes many calculations in his temple before the battle is fought. The general who loses makes but few calculations beforehand".[17] Preparation is the key to success. This often-used moniker is often used for a reason. He who's most prepared will give himself the best chance at success. What does preparation look like for us?

For starters, make sure that you have the correct time, date, courthouse, case, and room. All of this information should appear on the subpoena. When you received your subpoena, make sure that you have made the necessary scheduling arrangements in your calendar. Make contact with the prosecuting attorney and ask them for a quick update on the case prior to court. Ask them if anything is needed of you or how you can be of any assistance to them.

Frequently, prosecutors are overwhelmed and under a heavy caseload. Offering them a helping hand will not only get you in their good graces but reaffirms the fact that we're all on the same side. As the court date nears, make sure that you repeatedly review the case material. This includes event reports, supplements, witness statements, evidence, lab reports, and the like. For large cases, this will be crucial. The human memory can't take an overload of information all at once. The memory retention we have is not equipped to handle that level of information. Instead, give yourself two weeks or so of preparation time. Spend ten or fifteen minutes a day and go over the case details thoroughly. It's your duty to become an expert in the case at hand. The last thing you want to do appear unprepared in front of the judge or jury. This will lead to the perception that this case may not be of importance to you since you

---

[17] Sun Tzu Quotes. Quotes.net. STANDS4 LLC. Accessed May 9, 2016. http://www.quotes.net/quote/50877

could hardly be bothered to study up on the details. It will lead to the judge or jury having a negative opinion of you and it's not a good start.

As you are reviewing the case, objectively identify the strengths and weaknesses of your case. Look at the areas of your case that could be susceptible. Defense attorneys will almost always attack the reason for the stop in the first place. For if they can convince the judge or jury that their client was illegally stopped everything that happens after that can be susceptible to the exclusionary rule, and your case may be thrown out. Put your lawyer hat on and anticipate some of those issues during your preparation. Not only will it help you objectively review your case, but also if any of those issues are brought up in testimony, you will be prepared to explain your actions with thoughtful insight. I know this one is going to sound dumb, but review what you wrote in your reports. Frequently testimony occurs several months after the initial stop. Nothing is more embarrassing when the defense attorney quotes you verbatim from your report, and you didn't know it was you who wrote those words. Thoroughly read your reports and make sure you're familiar with the material you put in them. Now a quick disclaimer, there is such a thing as too much preparation. The only case of this is the day of the trial. By the time you reach the courthouse, you should be well attuned to your case. There's nothing wrong with a quick glance over at your notes, but hopefully, by then, you should've done all the preparing you need. Go ahead and grab some reading material for the time before court that is not associated with your case. It'll serve you well to clear your mind from the case beforehand. Grabbing additional non-case reading material will also give you some entertainment value while you sit in the waiting area for an unknown amount of time.

Perhaps one of the most overlooked aspects of preparing to testify in court is to ensure that you are reasonably well rested. Now it's easy to say, but in this career, the term "well rested" is more like a unicorn—often talked about but never seen. Even though you will spend most of this career deprived of sleep, you still need to make a commitment to get what sleep and rest you can when you can. If you go into court tired and irritable, you will not be sharp, and it will not lead to a positive outcome.

Dress for Success!

I know its lame and quite possibly one of the most overused phrases; however, it's very relevant to the topic at hand. If you have chosen to wear your duty or dress uniform, ensure that it is presentable. Anything that can be shined should be. Any lose strings should be removed. Your duty uniform should be pressed and neat in appearance. You want to portray the appearance of a professional police officer that knows what he's doing. First impressions are the best impressions and you want to leave a good impression on the judge and/or jury. Make no mistake if you want to send a clear message to all in the courtroom that you are a professional and deserve to be treated as such.

If you choose to wear a suit, make sure it, too, is presentable. Visually inspect beforehand to make sure any strings are cut lose and there are no stains. Make sure the shirt, tie, and shoes match. Most importantly, make sure that the suits fit. A lot of officers graduate the police academy and have dropped several clothes sizes. Make sure you get a few new suits to accommodate your new figure. You don't have to blow the budget to get a good quality suit. Many department stores have decent options, and there are many outlet retailers that carry suits now. You can get a nice, professional-looking suit for under $150. The importance of having a properly-fitted suit is obvious. It exudes professionalism. Nothing screams sloppy like a suit that is two sizes too big and is hanging off your body. From a psychological perspective, it also affords you both anonymity and mutual respect. In my experience, many lawyers will look down at police officers dressed in police uniforms. A nice suit lets them know that they're not the only ones that can dress nice. It has the psychological effect of letting the attorney know that you are on equal playing terms with them. In terms of anonymity, a suit lets you blend into the crowd at court. I can't tell you the amount of times that other individuals have approached me in court, asking this question or that because they see the uniform. Having a suit on makes it less likely you will be disrupted from your case or pulled into some other drama that could roll into you. Trust me, I've seen many court-room brawls, and it's the last thing anyone wants to deal with when they are preparing to testify.

Get Organized!

This will be a critical skill that you need to obtain to be successful as a police officer. We don't have the luxury of handling one case at a time. Throughout your career, you could have dozens, even scores of open court cases on your calendar at any given time. During your field-training program, you should develop organizational structures that work best for you to maintain your court caseload.

Always make sure you document the dates of your court appearances. Nowadays, everyone has a smartphone, so use it. Download or utilize the calendar function on your phone and ensure that with every subpoena, there's a corresponding calendar entry. Be sure to include pertinent information such as date, time, location, and case name or number (whatever will prompt your memory of the case). Since you went through all the effort of entering the dates in your device, make sure you review the calendar at least once a week to ensure that you're mentally prepared for your upcoming court appearances. As with any electronic device, our phones are prone to failure. It's essential that you maintain some alternate source of tracking and scheduling your court cases. The last thing you need is to lose access to your calendar and have angry attorneys calling you and the defendant walking free because you failed to appear in court. If you need to, get one of those small calendar or scheduling books to record your court dates. It will only take a few extra seconds, but the security and peace of mind that you have some kind of backup protocol in place is well worth the time.

Just as it's critical to organize your court dates, you must develop a system for maintaining your hard copy paperwork. This includes arrest reports, court subpoena, lab reports, property forms, and/or any other hard copy paperwork that will be pertinent to your case. While the fun stuff is what occurs on the patrol, maintaining and organizing the relevant information important to your case will prevent you untold numbers of headaches. I know it's old school, but the easiest way I've found is to utilize a plain, old file cabinet. You can create folders based on each case, and as you collect paperwork in regards to that case, you can simply insert it in your folder to ensure that all the case materials remain together. If you're looking for a more technology-friendly option, there are apps available that allow you to save picture files as PDFs. You can simply take a picture of the paperwork and transfer it to a desktop to be saved under a file created for that particular case. There are other options available that let you scan documents into computers and save them, allowing them to be easily retrieved at any time. Whatever method you choose, you will serve no good to the prosecution of your case if you can't stay organized.

The last prong of getting organized for court I want to discuss is often overlooked but nonetheless relevant. Make sure you obtain the pertinent contact information for the local prosecuting attorney's office, court liaison, clerk's office, and the like. Communication between officer and court is a critical component of a successful working relationship. Many departments have court liaison officers or offices. Get familiar with them. If possible, visit the courthouse during field training and get a sense for your court liaison office. Many resources are typically housed there from continuance forms, driving history, criminal history, room assignments, and other pertinent court information and forms. Know where your prosecutor's offices are located. There will be many other phone numbers and room assignments that you'll need to learn as your career progresses; make sure you take note of each and every one. This will include courtrooms or offices for prosecutions of specific types of cases from narcotics to sex offenses to weapons charges. Make sure you locate and are familiar with grand jury processes in your jurisdiction. Many times, grand juries may only be held on certain dates with different prosecutors and in different rooms. Familiarize yourself with those procedures.

Likewise, preliminary hearings and other pretrial functions may take place in different rooms or with different prosecutors. I can tell you unequivocally that juvenile prosecutors and courtrooms will certainly be different. Make sure you ascertain the locations and contact information for the juvenile courts, clerks, and prosecutors as well. Much like the juvenile system is separate, often so too are the criminal and civil courts. Again make sure to identify where each is located and obtain the contact information for each. I know it's dizzying and sometimes redundant, but there are many moving parts to the criminal justice system. We don't want to see our hard work unraveled because of a lack of communication or familiarity with any court process. Defense attorneys will take advantage of an imperfect system. Let's make sure that we do our due diligence to ensure that we're prepared and knowledgeable for all court related procedures. Depending on your activity level, it will take years for you to visit and experiences all of the different court-related experiences. You should take that as a challenge, and challenge yourself to become an expert in that area.

Fuel Up for the Day!

Since court can be an all-day ordeal, make sure in the morning, you partake in whatever breakfast time rituals you usually partake in. I've sat in court for hours on end, and the most depressing thing in the world is slumbering over to the vending machine on a grumbling stomach to discover it's out of order. The point is, if you are a breakfast person, eat breakfast, and if coffee is your morning tradition, grab a cup before you go in. Make sure you are prepared to sit there for eight hours if need be. Nothing is worse than sitting there on an empty stomach. The police career is unpredictable. I've been in court for five minutes; I've been in court for eight hours, so you must plan accordingly. Going into the courtroom with hunger pangs reverberating throughout your stomach is a recipe for disaster and can seriously affect your performance.

We're In

As you enter the courthouse and make your way to the appropriate room, make sure you check in with the prosecutor. This lets them know you're actually present. Also be sure to ask what the status of your case is. Oftentimes, you might enter the courthouse prepared to testify only to find that your case isn't proceeding either due to a continuance, a plea deal or some other reason. Checking in with the prosecutor and actively asking the status of the case can mitigate this. I've sat for too many hours in courtrooms only to have the prosecutor come out and ask me, "Why are you still here? We settled that hours ago." Nothing is more maddening than having wasted precious hours of your day sitting in a court waiting room only to find that for whatever reason you're not needed.

First Impressions Do Matter!

We are always told that first impressions matter because, of course, they do! It's important that anytime you're in the courthouse, whether it's on the stand, in the waiting area or in the bathroom you carry yourself with the expected decorum. You don't want to be telling off color jokes to the guy next to you in the bathroom only to have your heart drop when you enter the courtroom to testify and that same guy is the judge in your case. Judges, lawyers, and juries expect you to act with decorum and professionalism. You can do irreparable harm to your case by acting like a frat boy while in court. Your appearance in court is a serious matter, and you should treat it as such.

The individuals we encounter in court whether it's the judge or jury, already have in their mind how a police officer should carry him or herself. In many cases, you would have never before met any members of the jury, so it's important to make a great first impression. The first impression you want the jury left with is that they're dealing with a professional, competent, police officer. Portraying yourself in this manner will speak directly to your credibility, and that's one of the only currencies inside of a courtroom. If you're credible, and rightly perceived as such, it will give you an important psychological advantage with the fact finder. The defense attorney will spend a considerable amount of time trying to put your credibility in to question. Whether they're openly calling you a liar or trying the more subdued tactic of insinuating that you're just some hapless schmuck, credibility is your currency in front of the fact finding body.

The difference between winning and losing your case could simply hinge on the first impression you left with the jury, and you certainly want it to be positive. When entering the courtroom, walk with a purpose, stand erect but somewhat relaxed. Maintain good posture and exude the confidence that a professional police officer should. Even while sitting, you should maintain good posture. No fact finder wants the guy who's slouching and looking like he's waiting for a painful medical procedure to be the police officer that's testifying in his or her case. Like previously mentioned, people have a preconceived notion of what a police officer is and should look like, and we don't want to disappoint.

To the chagrin of a few in our career, part of your first impression is a proper greeting, and yes, this means to everyone. I'm not saying you have to warmly embrace your defendant or his attorney but a simple handshake, smile, or head nod can be sufficient. Remember, you want to impart neutrality on to yourself. A simple greeting to the opposing party can go a long way in the minds of the judge or jury. It shows mutual respect, humility, compassion, and is of general good manners, all of which will give you an early advantage with the fact finder. When greeting the individuals in the courtroom, use a clear, concise, and firm voice. This will exude command presence and overall good confidence.

When being called to testify, rise and walk to the witness bench confidently, and with purpose. When being sworn in raise your arm, making sure your elbow is at a ninety-degree angle, forearm perpendicular to the ceiling, palm flat, and firmly respond to person swearing you in. When seated, make sure you maintain good posture. Speak loudly enough to be heard but don't shout. If there is a microphone, adjust it accordingly. Place your hands on your lap, or leave them folded on the lectern. Do not fidget around with them. This excludes nervousness, and in the minds of the jury could lead them to question why you're so nervous in the first place. It'll be too easy for them to equate nervousness with untrustworthiness.

As you're testifying, make sure that you make eye contact with whomever you are addressing. You want to be as personal as possible with your audience. If the audience is a jury, make eye contact as you're testifying with each and every member. You don't have to stare at them but make them feel as though you're talking to them not at or through them. Likewise, make eye contact with the judge and attorneys. Eye contact exudes quiet confidence and that equates to credibility. Think of it this way: your daughter's date comes to the front door, greets you in a quiet voice, all the while looking down at the ground and never once making eye contact with you. Nerves, maybe, but what kind of a first impression are you left? In most cases, not a really positive one, and I'd be willing to bet your daughter will be staying home for the night.

Keep your non-verbal cues in mind. Refrain from touching your face, stroking your chin, running your hands through your hair, touching your mouth, and the like. These are all body language cues that could indicate deceptive behavior in the minds of the jury. Instead, keep a calm, even look on your face. Your goal is to maintain the same even facial expression throughout your testimony. If you feel the need to itch your face, make sure you do it in a very deliberate way to show the jury that it's not a nervous twitch or some subconscious body language signal but instead simply an itch.

First impressions matter, and before you even being to testify, you want to make sure the fact finder knows that this is a professional police officer appearing before them. You want to exude confidence but present yourself as a neutral presenter of the facts. Remember, credibility is your currency in the courtroom and a positive first impression is a great start.

Leave Your Ego in the Closet!

We have spoken thus far of all the items you should be doing, and all of the items you should be bringing to court, the one thing you do not need to bring is an ego. Simply put, leave it at home. We've been slowly building the image of a prepared, competent, professional police officer that's a mere neutral portrayer of the facts of your case. The surest way to tear down everything we have been building is to impart your own ego into your court appearance. I get it; you want to win and so do I, but winning takes a multifaceted approach. Perception is usually reality, and it's well documented that the perception of a large ego can be a put off to most people. The last thing you want the fact finder to be doing is imputing all the negative qualities and perceptions that having a large ego embodies.

Qualities like arrogant, cocky, and know-it-all are qualities we don't want in the minds of our fact finder. Remember, you are presenting yourself in front of body of individuals, you want to be perceived as confident, not arrogant, and putting your ego aside will go a long way toward accomplishing that goal.

Lawyers will be the first to tell you how schooled and educated they are. Don't take offense. In fact, many of the professionals in the courtroom will have attained a lot more schooling than you on paper. This means nothing. Yes, they have fancy degrees and inflated vocabularies, but there is no one in the courtroom more knowledgeable in your case than you. Oftentimes, officers feel as though they need to overcompensate in regards to their own intellectual abilities in the face of someone with more legal schooling. Fight that temptation. The courthouse is not the time or place to be flexing muscles with a lawyer to see whose smarter than who.

As previously stated, you want to appear neutral and in control the entire time in front of the fact finder. Maintain decorum and have a nice, even temperament. Defense attorneys will employ a lot of techniques to knock police officers off their game. Don't let it happen to you. Don't take testifying personal. This is why you see a lot of lawyers on different sides of cases out playing golf together later. They don't take it personal and neither should you. Now as a disclaimer, a lot of folks do take things personally, but my goal for you is for you to be better than that. It's easy to devolve into petulant games with the defendant attorney but resist the urge. They'll employ many different tactics from name-calling to charges of impropriety. Don't take the bait and don't take it personally. They, for whatever reason, have chosen to enter that career field. They'll do whatever they have to do to get their clients acquitted. In the course of the trial, they may say all sorts of sensational things, all the while trying to attack your credibility. News flash, that's what they get paid to do. Let them devolve into the mud.

Your goal is to remain in control of your emotions, present an even temperament, and calmly portray the facts of the case to the judge or jury. Do not lose your temper. Lawyers will attempt to rile you up in hopes that you spill the beans and start divulging information that you otherwise would not have. Don't take the bait. Remain stoic throughout your testimony. The last thing the jury needs to see is you losing your cool. The theatrics can be left to the lawyers. The high road is often the hardest road. It's much easier to capitulate in the face of adversity and get down in the mud than it is to take the high road and deliver a neutral, winning testimony. Remember your credibility is at stake. Let the jury be left with a sour taste of the defense attorney not you.

Tell Your Story

Okay, you've confidently approached the witness stand, you've been sworn in, your body language and general demeanor exude confidence. You have greeted all involved parties. Thus far, you have presented yourself as a neutral party simply waiting to present the facts of the case. The prosecutor asks you your first question and . . . you quickly ramble through a few, short, incoherent sentences and stop speaking to look around at all the lost, quizzical expressions on the faces of the judge or jury—your nightmare has come true.

Let's pump the breaks for a minute. Testifying is much like telling a story. Remember, most of the time, only two individuals in the courtroom were at the scene of the crime, you and the defendant. Don't take this for granted. While all the sights, sounds, and smells of the scene in question might be floating around in your head, the judge and jury were not at the scene of the crime. They have no idea what happened. It's your job to transport them there. You need to paint a clear picture of the events that took place. When you read a book, the author will take many paragraphs or pages to set the stage and you should too. Your goal is to take the listener of your "story" on a trip through time and back to the scene. Talk about the sights, sounds, and smells that you experienced. Use adjectives and descriptive language when testifying. Use a little voice inflection and tell your story. Sell your story. Don't simply state, "I approached the defendant and he was causing a disturbance." The judge or jury might not know what a disturbance is.

Furthermore, a disturbance could mean anything to anyone. Instead say what you saw: "As I approached the defendant, I could see that crowds of people were starting to gather. Many citizens with small children were whisking their children away and covering their children's ears because the language being used by the defendant was so inflammatory and obscene. I could see that the defendant's body was tense and his eyes were wildly darting from side to side as if under the influence of some kind of intoxicant. The defendant was standing on a newspaper box, which he flipped over and strewn all the contents of it around the immediate area."

You want to jury or fact finder to feel like your wife does when her favorite soap opera ends abruptly right before the big dramatic event, on the edge of their seat. Your job is to convince them through your words that the actions taken by the defendant were obvious. Bring the judge and jury along with you, let them feel, see, and experience what you did when you were on scene.

Loose Lips

While being descriptive as possible is important, don't confuse being descriptive with offering too much information. One of the defense attorney's primary objectives will be to bring you down a road he or she wants, which usually has nothing to do with the case or the guilt of their client. Defense attorneys are excellent at obfuscating and distracting the jury from the actual evidence. Don't fall trap to this. With both the defense attorney and the prosecutor, simply answer the question that was presented and nothing more.[18] It's the lawyer's job to extract more information out of you. This is true for both sides. Whether it's the defense attorney or the prosecutor, don't offer more up than what's being asked.

I was participating in a motion to suppress surrounding a case in which my partner arrested an individual that was in possession of PCP and marijuana. I had testified in the General District Court and the motion to suppress was denied. The motion was appealed to the Circuit Court where my partner was to testify. After my partner's testimony, he exited the courtroom followed closely behind by the prosecutor and I could hear them apologizing to each other, which usually is not a good sign. I asked my partner what the outcome was and he stated that the motion to suppress was granted. I asked him what he was apologizing to the prosecutor for and he proceeded to tell me that the defense attorney successfully was able to trap him and lead him down some line of testimony that was completely inconsequential to the case. Defense attorneys are

---

[18] Valerie VanBrocklin. Are you ready to testify? Posted October 23, 2007. Accessed March 14, 2016. https://www.policeone.com/legal/articles/1459523-Are-you-ready-to-testify/

experts at this. Make it easy for yourself and your case and stick to the question asked.

Take Your Time

Make sure as you are being asked a question you pause slightly, no more than two to three seconds at most. This will serve a dual purpose. Not only will it allow you to process what has been asked and start to formulate an appropriate answer it will also allow time for the prosecutor to object if need be. If the prosecutor or defense does object, simply don't start speaking, or if you started to speak, immediately cease speaking. Wait patiently, silently, and allow for the process to take its course. When instructed to continue, do so. It's important to keep control of your facial expression during the entirety of the trial, but definitely during an objection. Lawyers object for many reasons. It's not our job to know why, even if you do. Fight the urge to roll your eyes or let out a sigh, or show some other signs of annoyance. This will play poorly with the jury and give the sense that you are not taking that particular piece of the trial seriously.

Be an Authority on Your Case!

No one in the courtroom knows your case more intimately than you, so be an authority on your case. Go the extra mile. Make sure that you review the elements of each crime you've charged the defendant with. Make sure you know the nuisances of your case. If it's a domestic-related offense, know what a domestic relation is in your area. If you're appearing on a narcotics charge, do a little research on the narcotic or drug in question. Know a brief history of the drug, know the chemical components, know the street names, and know the street value. Send a message to the fact finder that you take this case seriously enough to go above and beyond.

Lawyers are excellent at finding inconsistences in the code and charging language. Among the first things they will do when meeting with their clients for the first time will review the crimes their clients have been charged with and make sure that all the elements of each crime are met. Preempt them, and during your trial prep review the specific codes. You need to become an expert on your case. It will look much better in front of the jury to hear you responding with knowledgeable, confident answers. This also lets the defense attorney know that you have studied up and have done your due diligence by researching the pertinent details of your case. The court will generally put a lot of weight behind the experience level of the officer. This is especially true in grand jury hearings. They expect you to be knowledgeable on the subject matter.

If You Don't Know, You Don't Know

Remember that thing I told you to leave home? In case you forgotten, it's your ego. This is doubly important when testifying. When being questioned during trial, don't be afraid to say "I don't know." Contrary to what my wife would say, there's no person on the face of the earth that knows everything. I don't care how smart you are or how much experience you have; there will always be something that you don't know. If you're confronted with this at trial, utter those three simple words: "I don't know." There's nothing wrong with not knowing everything.

As previously mentioned, your goal is to be an expert on your case. You'll eventually be presented with a question from the defense attorney that you either don't know or are unsure of. If that's the case, it's okay. You can save a lot of credibility in front of the fact finder by admitting when you don't know something. Defense attorneys will often play on your ego and try and get you to go down a road of testimony that they know you'll be unsure of only to drop a bomb on you later on. Don't fall into this trap. End the perilous journey down that road before it even begins by being honest up front. The last thing you need is for some piece of evidence or testimony down the road to be brought up and not only impeach your testimony but lead to possible disciplinary action against you because your ego got in the way.

Remember credibility is your only currency. A fact finder doesn't want to listen to some pompous fool all day proclaiming to know everything under the sun. Connect with your jury. Let them know that your number one goal is preserving the utmost integrity in the system. History is littered with police officers that have been dismantled this way. Don't let it happen to you.

Listen Carefully!

Lawyers will oftentimes try to talk around in circles, making what they're asking you at times seem ambiguous. This is an often-used strategy that's employed when they are going on fishing expeditions. It's also a useful technique you can employ during person stops, but we've covered that already. Simply put, if you don't understand the question or vocabulary used ask for a clarification, make sure it's crystal clear in your mind what the defense attorney is asking you. Ask them to repeat the question. Ask them to rephrase the question if necessary. If it's easier for you to process, repeat the question that the defense wants answered back to them just for clarification. Listening and slowing down will also allow the prosecutor to step in when need be. Remember, there's no timetable for your testimony. Your goal is to make sure due process is served faithfully. Don't rush through questions or answers. Slow down, take your time, and listen carefully.

It's about Time

Lawyers will split hairs when it comes to certain details like distance and time. They'll try to attack your recollections of the event and try and tie that to your credibility. Don't get caught up on inconsequential distances and specific amounts of time that have passed.[19] Lawyers love to go round and round in front of the jury on this issue because they try and equate these issues to your credibility. Do the best you can with what you have.

I was never a big, specific distance guy. Even in the woods during hunting season, I was always off on the distances. Does this make me any less reliable of a witness? Of course not; do your best to explain the circumstances and make it clear that it's just an estimate. Oftentimes, lawyers will try and put words in your mouth regarding this topic. You'll hear statements like "Isn't it correct that the distance between you and the defendant was this…" If they are correct, state yes; if they are not correct, correct them. I often will use references in the courtroom to help the jury visualize for themselves. It's easy to say "The approximate distance between us was ten yards or the distance between counsel and the jury box."

---

[19] The Clark County Prosecuting Attorney. Effective Courtroom Performance by Indiana Law Enforcement. Accessed March 14, 2016. http://www.clarkprosecutor.org/html/police/police2.htm

You can also use adjectives to aid you in this. If you're being cross-examined in a case where you stopped an individual that had the odor of marijuana emanating from the defendant's person, it might sound something like this: "I was within arm's distance of the defendant, without anyone else in between us. I could smell the odor of marijuana emanating from the defendant's person. I was close enough to smell the defendant's breath."

Use visualization and descriptors to aid the jury with estimates regarding distance. As far as the passage of time, do the best you can. I've been on scenes where ten minutes feel like an hour and vice versa. Again, don't get hung up on arguing about whether it was ten seconds or twenty seconds. Make it perfectly clear it was an estimate. As with distance, describe it in such a manner that lets the judge or jury visualize it. "It was approximately ten seconds or the amount of time it took for me to walk from here to there before I stopped your client."

Again this allows the jury to visualize the scene and judge for themselves in their own minds how much time that could take.

Worry about Yourself!

Testifying to your actions is the only thing you should be doing while on the stand. Oftentimes, defense attorneys will try asking you about the actions or motivations of some other person whether it be an officer or the defendant. The appropriate answer is that you can't accurately testify to what someone else thought. You are not a psychic. You cannot read minds.

Do not go down the road of trying to psychoanalyze the mind frames of individuals, good or bad. Politely state that you can't testify to the internal motivations of that person. Now actions that you saw others commit are fair game and should be answered accordingly. Don't channel your inner Sigmund Freud. Stick to what you know.

Tell the Truth!

The most fundamental principle when it comes to testifying, and for that matter, all of police work, is to *tell the truth*, especially when on the stand. Committing perjury is a sure way to get you fired and criminally charged. History is littered with examples of cops perjuring themselves. No one remembers when a police officer gives excellent testimony crucial to getting a conviction. Everyone remembers when a police officer lies on the stand.

Don't put your integrity as well as the integrity of the entire profession in jeopardy. Many officers get themselves in trouble in regards to this when they start to go down the road of defending an indefensible position. If you've made a mistake, and it's brought out in testimony, just fess up and take responsibility. The cover up is always worse than the crime. You may lie to cover some inconsequential detail up, but if discovered, it will scuttle your entire credibility and most likely the entire case. The jury can sympathize with an officer that made a mistake in collecting evidence or a mistake in the chronological order of certain events. They will not forgive a police officer that openly lies. As far as the actions of others, let them speak for themselves. If you are trying to "cover up" for another, don't. Let them answer for their actions. Simply answer the questions politely, good or bad. Remember, by the time we get to court, all the legwork on the case is typically over. What has already happened in terms of the nuts and bolts of the stop is history and cannot be changed. You're simply there to state the facts of the case as they have already occurred. Don't jeopardize our entire profession because you don't want to fess up to some silly mistake. Everyone makes mistakes. No case is perfect. So if you find yourself in a precarious position, simply do the right thing by telling the truth. No amount of embarrassment suffered at taking responsibility for your actions will be worse than the shame and humiliation you'll suffer if you perjure yourself. Remember, credibility is the only currency.

Let's Sum It Up

In closing, you will not win every case. That super competitive person inside you loves to win, and that is an excellent characteristic to have, but at some point, you will lose. It's okay, regroup, learn from your mistakes, and move on. Some of your best learning experiences will come from your losses. The important thing is that you learn from your mistakes and work them into your learning curve so it doesn't happen next time. If the defendant is found not guilty, so be it. You'll get him another time.

I've run into multiple individuals multiple times. A truly guilty person will not get away with criminal actions forever. Don't get frustrated with the legal system. It's an imperfect system. Our job is to deliver defendants to the justice system. It's the justice system's job to do the rest. Every courtroom I've ever been in has been packed. We police officers are doing our jobs, and that's all that matters. Just like everything else, you need practice and experience to excel in this field. Get some reading material on strategies lawyers employ during cross-examination. It'll be very helpful and offer excellent insight. While you are sitting in court waiting for your case, watch, learn, and experience through the eyes of other officers. Listen to their testimony. Analyze what you did and didn't like. Remember some catch phrases that you might use in your own testimony. In this case, practice like a backup quarterback. You might not be in the game but run yourself through the mental reps. Envision yourself up there on the stand, taking questions and formulating answers. This is not a natural skill, but it soon will be. With practice and experience together, you will learn to excel in the courtroom.

CHAPTER

11

Internal Investigations

One of the most unsettling and stressful experiences for any officer is being investigated. Depending on the temperament, policies, and procedures, it seems as though in today's society, police officers will be investigated for anything. Investigations can start from citizen's complaints, video footage, internal inquiries, supervisors, other officers, and anywhere else in between. When a formal investigation is conducted against you, it's a serious matter. Penalties can range from administrative discipline (from verbal counseling to termination), to civil, to criminal repercussions.

Will many of the investigations or complaints we receive be unmerited or unfair? Yes. However, there's little we can do about it. In the nature of today's world, with lawyers crawling over everything, many departments will investigate all accusations just to protect themselves from liability. Remember, just because you received a complaint or are being investigated doesn't mean that you did anything wrong. As you get out on patrol and start conducting stops, you will learn that it will be only a matter of time before you receive a complaint that leads to an investigation. If you make stops, you will get complaints, period. Don't take it personal. As long as you are doing what you are supposed to be, the right way, you will be fine.

It's important that you learn the rules and procedures surrounding your department's internal affairs divisions. Make sure you understand what's required of them and what's required of you when being investigated or making statements. If you have a union, become familiar with their responsibilities to you and their procedures for handling complaints and investigations against officers. If you don't have a union, make sure you become familiar with the labor laws in your area. Remember, just because you're being investigated doesn't mean you did anything wrong, but you should still take the process seriously.

I want to share with you a few guidelines you can employ when you're required to make a written statement. Keep in mind you need to follow whatever procedures are in place in your department. If you feel as though you could be the subject of a criminal investigation consult with a lawyer. However, if you're being investigated and asked to provide a written statement in response, here are a few tips to help you construct a proper statement. This list is by no means conclusive, and make sure before providing any statement, that you consult with another person that's familiar with the protocols surrounding investigations in your department whether it be another officer, a union representative, or a lawyer.

If you are required to provide a written statement:

Collect your thoughts and remain calm, cool, and collected. Resist the urge to immediately respond. Instead, listen to what the official is stating and what will be required from you. Gather your thoughts and ask follow-up questions to the official regarding the statement. Control your emotions and prepare to deliver a concise statement.

Take the accusation, complaint, or statement seriously.

If you are ordered to write a statement, disciplinary action can follow regardless of the nature of the alleged offense. Any written statement can lead to an investigation, which in turn can lead to disciplinary action up to and including termination. Don't make the mistake of believing the subject in which you're writing on is inconsequential. Take every statement seriously and be prepared to defend your actions.

Know what you're being accused of.

Many officials will ask you to write a "blanket" statement regarding the offense. Make sure you ask the official requiring you to write the statement what specifically you're being accused of. This will better allow you to tailor the statement toward what you're being accused of. This will eliminate officials going on a fishing expedition in search of violations that otherwise might not have come up.

If you're being required to write a statement based on a citizen complaint, inquire what the specific complaint is. If you are being required to write a statement on a procedural violation, inquire specifically which ones you are being accused of violating.

Take your time.

Resist the urge to hastily write your statement. Your statement could be the difference between being fired and retaining your job, so it deserves to be taken seriously and have the appropriate amount of time devoted to it. Do not rush, take the time to proofread, and edit your work. If possible have a union representative or another officer who you trust proofread your work.

Know your general orders or SOPs and reference them if possible.

In many cases, when being ordered to write a statement, the accusations and subsequent investigation will center on violations of general orders. Know which general orders you're accused of violating, and if possible, reference pertinent general orders in your statement. Many general orders are open to interpretation. If that's the case, also include your reasonable interpretations of the referenced general order.

Know when you're right; know when you're wrong.

When defending your position, make sure you back up your positions with evidence. Research each point and be sure when you're arguing a point, you know it is correct and you can back it up with the appropriate evidence.

On the other hand, if you know the position is wrong, do not waste your time defending it. It's far better to concede a losing point than to surrender credibility defending a faulty position. If this is the case, instead of focusing on the specific point, focus on framing the narrative of the position. Show that even though what you did may have been not in accordance with some procedure, what you did was ultimately reasonable. Make sure you explain this in a clear and concise manner and frame your point with the veil of "reasonableness."

Tell the truth.

The truth is the most powerful part of your statement. It's far better to tell the truth and explain why you did what you did than to lie. Many officers will lie about inconsequential issues, only to be fired for the actual lying than the original offense. The cover-up is always worse than the crime. Individuals can sympathize with an individual that made a mistake and took responsibility for it. No one will sympathize with someone that has blatantly lied.

Be as precise as possible when detailing your statement.

Your statement should emulate an arrest narrative. It should tell your story or position as clearly and concisely as possible. It should be written in such a manner that the reader need not have been present at the scene, but by merely reading it, they can envision him or herself in your shoes. The goal is for them understand the complete situation without the need to ask you follow-up questions. Being as precise and clear as possible will give credibility to your statement and mitigate the recipient of your statement from believing you're omitting the truth.

Offer reasons.

If you are being required to write a statement regarding a procedural violation or non-complaint issue, offer reasons as to why you did what you did. Explain in a clear and concise manner what your reasoning for doing what you did was. Your goal is to transport the reader into your decision-making process and let them feel and experience what you did when you made your choice.

If you have to write a statement because you called out on the radio after given an order to limit radio traffic. State in your statement why you did it.

For example, you were training an FTO and had to balance training needs, or if the offense were so blatant that to ignore it would tarnish the integrity of the department, etc.

Just the facts.

When writing your statement, remember to be objective and offer only facts and evidence. Resist the urge to offer your opinion. Offering your opinion will only lead to you sounding defensive. You don't want to be conclusive with your opinion. Let the evidence, not your opinion, lead the reader to your side of the argument. If your evidence is strong and your argument well-crafted, the reader will naturally move to your position.

Offer rebuttals to the complainant.

If an individual is accusing you of a specific complaint offer direct rebuttals, explain the reasoning behind why you did what you did. If an accusation that is made against you is false, state quite clearly that it's false, and instead, offer the correct version of events. This only holds true if there is a contradiction in something you said or did. If the complaint is an ambiguous complaint of racism, sexism, or some other discriminatory complaint, don't spend time in your statement explaining why you are not those things. Explaining why you're not something will just come across as defensive. You will never be able to explain why you're not something. Instead, focus on the actions you took and what was actually said. Make sure the reader understands the motivations underlying the actions you took. For example, if you are accused of stopping an individual because of their race, instead of stating that you didn't profile them or stop them because of their race, explain why you stopped them and whether you had reasonable suspicion or probable cause for the stop. This will allow the reader to understand why you stopped them and will dispel any underlying charges of impropriety.

Offer a closing.

A statement should include a proper closing. Use the last paragraph of your statement to summarize the statement and offer a "personal statement." It should be short and to the point. The purpose is to cement your statement and leave a lasting impression in the mind of the reader. Be purposeful and really use it to grip the reader and sound as genuine and persuasive as possible.

CONCLUSION

A Few Parting Words

In this new age of policing, the stakes could not be higher. The media and police naysayers lie in wait behind every corner ready to yell "Gotcha!" and to shine a light on those evil police officers. Well, newsflash media and naysayers, what you're looking for just isn't there. Show the naysayer that behind that badge on your chest is something more, something a little more special, something that can't be broken and will not back down. We always hear in the weight room that our goal is to become bigger, faster, and stronger than the next.

Well, I full heartedly agree I would like to modify that saying for what we, as police officers need to become. We need to become bigger, faster, stronger, and smarter. We need to train our minds as well as our body. We need to understand that we can no longer try to ram the square peg into the circle hole. The one size fits all mentality will not help us meet the new challenges that we face. We need to adapt and employ multiple different strategies according to what the situation calls for. We need to be fast thinking and witty on our feet. We need to learn the laws we enforce, admit when we're wrong, and take the appropriate corrective action. We need to learn to drive the narrative of a stop, encounter, or citizen interaction. By driving the narrative, we need to flip the current mentality of society and make them realize once more that the persons that should be drawing their ire aren't police officers but those among them that wish them harm, those among them that would steal their property, those among them that would infest their streets and their children with dangerous drugs, and those among them with evil intentions.

JEREMY GUIDA

Help the citizen once more see that it's the criminal that's responsible for his actions and it's the criminal in most cases that's leading to the decay of some of these areas. Help the citizen once more understand that they should demand that those individuals be routed out of their neighborhoods. Remind the citizen that we need and want the help of communities throughout the country to rout out and deliver these individuals to justice. No one will lose an ounce of sleep if the criminally responsible among us are held accountable for his or her actions. Only after we rid society of these individuals can we start to heal and rebuild the neighborhoods that they have destroyed. We need to band together citizen and police officer and do our country a service. It'll be up to you to carry this message. And you can do so with some of the tips that you learned in this book.

Change the way you interact with citizens and criminals alike. Put your ego and emotions to the side when making your decisions or interacting with people. Appeal to their rational side and show them why what you're doing is the morally sensible thing to do. You will not win over every person, but you'll win over most and that's a start in the right direction. My goal for you is to see the big picture before you even make a stop. Start to craft in your head the legal issues that could arise, questions you might ask the person, questions that might be asked of you, what you will asked during trial, and the like. We always hear about always trying to be one step ahead, while I want you to be ten steps ahead. Know what the criminal will do before they do it. Use some of the body language indicators we discussed and buy yourself more reaction time. End dangerous encounters before they even become dangerous by paying attention to what we've discussed. Be smarter, and it will make you safer. Likewise, when you're dealing with citizens, we also need to be ten steps ahead. Before you say or do something, start to think of how it will be perceived. Learn to strategize and counter arguments by the other person before they are even made. Craft your message and allow the public to see you at your best. Allow them to see nothing but the positive. The very best level of policing that their tax dollars will buy should be you.

Once you employ some of these techniques we've discussed, you will notice something different. You'll notice the way you interact with the public and with criminals has changed. You'll start to see things that others miss. You'll start to visualize and conceptualize arguments made by others before they are even made you'll start to be ten steps ahead. You'll start to make arrests that others aren't. You'll see that the quality and the outcomes of your stops will increase exponentially. You'll notice that your arrests, though slightly fewer, will increase in quality. You'll evolve into what you always thought you were, *a proven police officer.*

In closing, trust your instincts. The more stops you make, the more experience you'll garner. The more experience you garner, the safer you'll be able to make your stops. As you develop those instincts, learn to trust them. The little guy on your shoulder is never wrong and should not be ignored. If something feels wrong, it's probably wrong, so correct it.

Remember the big picture. Remember that we're here to deliver individuals to justice the proper and legal way. Nothing matters if we cheat the rules. We could get the best arrest on the face of the earth, but if we betray our integrity to achieve it, we have only achieved disgrace. In this ever-changing world, we need to be ever-adapting. We need to turn different areas on and off as we move in and out of ever-changing scenes. We need to redefine and drive the narrative that police officers are to be looked up to and admired, not scorned. We need to drive the narrative and remind the public that there are wolves among them and our very reason for existence is to rout those wolves out so that others may live in peace.

Remember the citizens you swore to protect, the constitution you swore to uphold, and the communities you swore to serve. *Non Timebo Mala!* Now get out there and become proven!

Show the world you're proven! Help others learn from your experiences. Join us on social media at ProvenPolice.

REFERENCES

Darrin Weiner. FBI Findings on Cop Killers. Posted April 04, 2013. Accessed April 18, 2016. www.Calgunlaws.com/fbi-finds-on-cop-killers/

Chuck Remsburg. Traits That Get Cops Killed. Accessed April 18, 2016. http://www.poam.net/train-and-educate/2008/train-educate/

Francis Clines. Police Killers Offer Insights into Victim's Fatal Mistakes. Posted March 9, 1993. Accessed April 18, 2016. http://nytimes.com/1993/03/09/us/police-killers-offer-insights-into-victims-fatal-mistakes.html

Findlaw. Mapp v. Ohio. Accessed March 29, 2016. http://caselaw.findlaw.com/us-supreme-court/367/643.html

Legal Information Institute. Terry v. Ohio. Accessed March 29, 2016. https://www.law.cornell.edu/supremecourt/text/392/1

Findlaw. Reasonable Suspicion. Accessed May 2, 2016. http://dictionary.findlaw.com/definition/reasonable-suspicion.html

Legal Information Institute. Minnesota v. Dickerson. Accessed March 28, 2016. https://www.law.cornell.edu/supct/html/91-2019.ZO.html

Findlaw. Probable Cause. Accessed May 2, 2016.

http://criminal.findlaw.com/criminal-rights/probable-cause.html

Justia. Illinois v. Gates. Accessed March 29, 2016. https://supreme.justia.com/cases/federal/us/462/213/

Legal Information Institute. Fourth Amendment. Accessed May 2, 2016. https://www.law.cornell.edu/constitution/fourth_amendment

Ted Belling. Search Warrant Exemptions. Accessed March 29, 2016. http://www.caselaw4cops.net/articles/exceptions.html

Ray Sanchez. Oklahoma Police Officer's Body-Cam Captures Fatal Shooting. Posted January 24, 2015. Accessed May 10, 2016. http://www.cnn.com/2015/01/23/us/oklahoma-police-shooting-video/index.html

Sun Tzu Quotes. Quotes.net. STANDS4 LLC. Accessed May 9, 2016. http://www.quotes.net/quote/50877

Valerie VanBrocklin. Are you ready to testify? Posted October 23, 2007. Accessed March 14, 2016. https://www.policeone.com/legal/articles/1459523-Are-you-ready-to-testify/

The Clark County Prosecuting Attorney. Effective Courtroom Performance by Indiana Law Enforcement. Accessed March 14, 2016. http://www.clarkprosecutor.org/html/police/police2.htm

CPSIA information can be obtained
at www.ICGtesting.com
Printed in the USA
BVOW04s1150161216

471030BV00012B/98/P